T0299284

The Endowment Effect and Housing Markets

This book aims to provide a comprehensive analysis of the so-called "endowment effect" in the housing market. In a nutshell, the phenomenon of overvaluing things we own which was first conceptualised in 1980 and has since been one of the most studied behavioural biases in economics.

The first chapter presents a systematic review of the literature on the endowment effect in the housing market, together with the identification of research gaps to be filled by other researchers. The second chapter aims to propose a theoretical model explaining the strength of the endowment effect in sales and rental housing markets by primary and secondary markets. The last chapter presents the results of empirical research on the endowment effect in the Polish housing market, testing the model presented in Chapter 2. The chapters can be read together or independently by researchers, students, and policymakers interested in behavioural economics in housing and real estate. For policymakers, the book can be extremely useful as the endowment effect can create friction in the housing market because of a mismatch between the price demands of sellers and buyers, especially in countries where the level of market professionalisation is low (such as Poland). Thanks to the empirical research contained in this book, it will be possible to identify specific market segments where the endowment effect may be particularly elevated – on such segments, policymakers should introduce actions contributing to the elimination of this behavioural bias.

Mateusz Tomal is an assistant professor in the Department of Real Estate and Investment Economics at the Krakow University of Economics. His research interests include housing markets, real estate economics, behavioural economics, econometric modelling, spatial analysis, and local government efficiency.

Routledge Studies in International Real Estate

The Routledge Studies in International Real Estate series presents a forum for the presentation of academic research into international real estate issues. Books in the series are broad in their conceptual scope and reflect an inter-disciplinary approach to Real Estate as an academic discipline.

Residential Satisfaction and Housing Policy Evolution
Clinton Aigbavboa and Wellington Thwala

International Housing Market Experience and Implications for China
Edited by Rebecca L. H. Chiu, Zhi Liu and Bertrand Renaud

Interests and Behaviours of Real Estate Market Actors in Commercial Property Valuation
Alina Nichiforeanu

New Frontiers in Real Estate Finance
The Rise of Micro Markets
Patrick Lecomte

Marxism and Real Estate Development
Taking Lefebvre for developers seriously
Julian Roche

The Endowment Effect and Housing Markets
Theory and Evidence from Poland
Mateusz Tomal

The Endowment Effect and Housing Markets

Theory and Evidence from Poland

Mateusz Tomal

Routledge
Taylor & Francis Group

LONDON AND NEW YORK

First published 2025
by Routledge
4 Park Square, Milton Park, Abingdon, Oxon OX14 4RN

and by Routledge
605 Third Avenue, New York, NY 10158

Routledge is an imprint of the Taylor & Francis Group, an informa business

© 2025 Mateusz Tomal

The right of Mateusz Tomal to be identified as author of this work has been
asserted in accordance with sections 77 and 78 of the Copyright, Designs and
Patents Act 1988.

All rights reserved. No part of this book may be reprinted or reproduced or utilised
in any form or by any electronic, mechanical, or other means, now known or
hereafter invented, including photocopying and recording, or in any information
storage or retrieval system, without permission in writing from the publishers.

Trademark notice: Product or corporate names may be trademarks or
registered trademarks, and are used only for identification and explanation
without intent to infringe.

British Library Cataloguing-in-Publication Data
A catalogue record for this book is available from the British Library

Library of Congress Cataloging-in-Publication Data
Names: Tomal, Mateusz, author.
Title: The endowment effect and housing markets: theory and evidence
    from Poland / Mateusz Tomal.
Description: Abingdon, Oxon; New York, NY : Routledge, 2025. |
    Series: Routledge studies in international real estate | Includes
    bibliographical references and index.
Identifiers: LCCN 2024026259 (print) | LCCN 2024026260 (ebook) |
    ISBN 9781032833385 (hardback) | ISBN 9781032842752
    (paperback) | ISBN 9781003512004 (ebook)
Classification: LCC HD1390.5 .T66 2024 (print) | LCC HD1390.5 (ebook) |
    DDC 333.33/8—dc23/eng/20240614
LC record available at https://lccn.loc.gov/2024026259
LC ebook record available at https://lccn.loc.gov/2024026260

ISBN: 978-1-032-83338-5 (hbk)
ISBN: 978-1-032-84275-2 (pbk)
ISBN: 978-1-003-51200-4 (ebk)

DOI: 10.1201/9781003512004

Typeset in Times New Roman
by Apex CoVantage, LLC

The data that support the findings of this study are openly available in RODBUK
at https://doi.org/10.58116/UEK/WP1MAC, UNF:6:CRZah9SWz2CSA2z36
cKWVQ==.

Contents

Figures

Tables

Acknowledgements

I would like to thank two anonymous reviewers for their valuable comments on an earlier version of the book. I would also like to thank the Krakow University of Economics for funding the research presented in Chapter 3.

Introduction

The essence of behavioural economics

Economics can be defined as science that deals with the creation of theories to better understand the reality around us by explaining the relationships between economic phenomena (Wilkinson & Klaes, 2017). Currently, the primary economic theory is the neoclassical model. In microeconomic terms, this model assumes that an individual, during the decision-making process, is rational, fully informed, has stable preferences, and ultimately seeks to maximise his or her utility/profit. However, mainstream economics has been criticised for many years because of restrictive assumptions that are too distant from reality, limiting its explanatory power (Folmer, 2009). On these foundations, behavioural economics was developed, which relaxes the principles of neoclassical economics by drawing on various disciplines of the social sciences, particularly economics and psychology. Consequently, behavioural economics attempts to explain economic phenomena broadly (Wilkinson & Klaes, 2017). Earl (2005) points out that behavioural economics uses inputs from psychology to better understand and more accurately predict human decisions. Specifically, behavioural economics studies all aspects of economic decision-making, particularly the nature of human preferences, their cognitive processes, and the mechanisms affecting them (Mallard, 2016). Further, Folmer (2009) indicates that, according to the behavioural school, people rely on perceptions, expectations, and habits when making decisions, and that their preferences vary according to changes in intrinsic motivation. However, current behavioural researchers do not attempt to completely replace mainstream economics but rather add more realistic assumptions to it (Camerer & Loewenstein, 2004; Ho et al., 2006). What also distinguishes behavioural economics from mainstream economics is the

DOI: 10.1201/9781003512004-1

type of methods used. The latter is dominated by quantitative models, whereas the former supplements these models with experimental approaches (Baddeley, 2019).

It is important to stress that behavioural economics is not a single economic theory, but rather a collection created over the years. Sent (2004) distinguishes three phases in the development of behavioural economics: (i) the period of old behavioural economics, (ii) the period of transition between old and new behavioural economics, and (iii) the period of new behavioural economics. Within old behavioural economics, Sent (2004) highlights four groups of researchers. The first and most important of these centred around Simon's (1957) theory of bounded rationality, according to which humans do not seek to maximise their utility/profit during the decision-making process but choose the first satisfactory solution under the given criteria. The second group gathered around George Katona, returned to psychological analysis and attempted to use the ideas of cognitive psychology to explain the process of learning individuals from groups. Like Simon (1957), Katona (1975) questioned the rationality of the individual, claiming that human beings are influenced by their experiences, norms, attitudes, and habits. Katona (1975) emphasised that the decision-making process is influenced by group membership, which links sociology and behavioural economics. Katona's (1975) research also highlighted that people use shortcuts and rules of thumb, and behave in repetitive ways (Hosseini, 2011). A third group of representatives of old behavioural economics focused on the analysis of economic decisions in the face of uncertainty (for example, Marschak (1950)), and the last was on integrationism and eclecticism. In summary, old behavioural economics tried to explain how people deal with complex decisions, given that individuals have a limited capacity to process information (Earl & Littleboy, 2014). However, it never became part of the "proper" economics because it consciously distanced itself from it (Sent, 2004).

The transition period between old and new behavioural economics began in the 1970s, mainly through the research of Amos Tversky, Daniel Kahneman, and Richard Thaler. In contrast to studies on bounded rationality, the researchers of new behavioural economics took the assumptions of neoclassical economics as a benchmark and then studied deviations from it to explain cognitive mechanisms (Camerer, 1999). The main contributions of Tversky and Kahneman to new behavioural economics were the conceptualisation of heuristics, cognitive biases, and prospect theory. Heuristics can be defined as mental shortcuts that help in making decisions and judgements that require the processing of a large amount of information, thus enabling complex problems to be solved quickly. However, such actions may lead to biased decisions (Dale, 2015). Tversky and Kahneman (1974) proposed heuristics of availability, representativeness, and anchoring and adjustment. The first involves attributing a greater probability to events that are easily recalled in the memory. The second concerns making judgements based on analogies and stereotypes. The third involves estimating by beginning at a certain starting point (anchoring), which is then adjusted upward or downward (adjustment). However, it seems that a more important contribution to the behavioural literature during its transition period was the creation of the prospect theory of Kahneman and Tversky (1979) which, according to Mallard (2016), constituted behavioural economics as a distinct sub-discipline of economics. Prospect theory is concerned with decisions under risk and assumes that people evaluate the outcomes of a decision in relation to a reference point and frame them as gains or losses, with the latter weighing more than the former. Prospect theory also assumes that people are risk-averse with respect to gains and risk-seeking with respect to losses because they want to avoid them (Tomal & Brzezicka, 2023). Building on Tversky and Kahneman, Thaler attempted to assess the effects of using heuristics on decision-making, as well as the implications of prospect theory in situations where choices were not considered risky (Earl, 2018). Among other things, he identified the so-called endowment effect, which is a cognitive bias according to which people generally demand more to give up goods in their ownership than they would be willing to pay to acquire them. Thaler (1980) explained this effect on the basis of inferences from prospect theory; that is, removing a good from someone's endowment results in a loss and adding it results in a gain. Thaler also contributed to new behavioural economics by creating the theory of mental accounting and co-creating the concept of libertarian paternalism with Cass Sunstein (Neszveda, 2018).

Finally, the development of new behavioural economics began in the 1990s, during which the focus was on identifying alternative theories to explain apparent anomalies and pointing out that market forces, including competition or arbitrage, do not overcome human limitations. Sent (2004) explains that new behavioural economics seeks to largely formalise its theories within economic models. All of this leads some researchers to conclude that new behavioural economics is already part of the mainstream, as it generally retains the basics of rationality models while supplementing them with special considerations that take into account behavioural biases (Kahneman, 2003). Consequently, economists increasingly use the behavioural perspective to explain economic phenomena. This book addresses the endowment effect and the housing market, which, due to its size, is an important factor shaping the economy and an extremely interesting object of study for behavioural economists (Camerer & Loewenstein, 2004).

Behavioural economics and the housing market

The decision-making process in the housing market is complex. Housing decisions are among the most important in many people's lives because of the high capital intensity of real estate. Consequently, it would seem that, given the importance of these decisions, housing market participants are rational and act in line with the assumptions of neoclassical economics. According to the latter, decisions in the housing market aim to maximise the utility of housing buyers or the profits of housing producers (Gibb, 2009). However, the usefulness of mainstream economics is beginning to be questioned in the context of studying housing market behaviour, as many quantitative analyses in this area are unsatisfactory (Leung, 2004), and only by incorporating behavioural concepts does their explanatory power increase (Marsh & Gibb, 2011).

Boelhouwer (2011) points out that one example of combining behavioural phenomena with neoclassical economics is the inclusion of a lagged dependent variable on the right-hand side of the equation in standard house price models, which makes it possible to consider the speculative behaviour of consumers. Similarly, Smith (2011) specifies that mainstream economics has problems explaining house price dynamics. Within the neoclassical school, house price models are based on Rosen's (1974) hedonic price theory, according to which buyers and sellers are willing to transact at the market price, which is derived from a hedonic function. The latter specifies the relationship between the price of a dwelling and its utility-bearing characteristics. In this approach, transacting parties are rational, and house prices are determined by their attributes, mediated by market fundamentals that affect housing supply and demand. However, Smith (2011) postulates that this view is far from sufficient because house prices may depend on "anchors" (e.g. neighbouring property prices) or contextual effects.

Dunning (2017) emphasises that behavioural housing research incorporating the influence of heuristics and biases situates it within new behavioural economics. In this framework, a housing market participant attempts to maximise utility/profit but has incomplete information, limited capacity to process it, and makes decisions through heuristics, which can lead to cognitive biases. For example, analysing real estate prices from Arizona (USA), Horenstein et al. (2017) found that out-of-town residential property buyers tend to pay more for similar assets, which may be due to decision-making based on the availability heuristic. This results from the fact that out-of-town buyers often view a property for purchase only once, and at that time, it is in a condition and standard that will maximise its sale. By contrast, in-town buyers may give more thought to the purchase decision, which leads to more rational choices. In turn, Cascão et al. (2023) found evidence that the decision-making process of investors in the Portuguese housing market is influenced by the representativeness heuristic. Specifically, investors assess the probability of a housing market event based on their similarity with the data at their disposal. The anchoring heuristic is also documented empirically in the housing literature. For example, Leung and Tsang (2013) identified that buyers in the Hong Kong housing market anchored the previous purchase price of a property. Kokot (2023), on the other hand, while studying the real estate market in Poland, found that market participants anchor themselves on the price level ingrained in their minds. Furthermore, Malik et al. (2021) provided some evidence that real estate prices may be influenced by overconfidence, the herding effect, gamblers' fallacy, and regret aversion. Next, Levy et al. (2020) empirically proved that prices in the housing market increase or decrease following the portrayal of the market situation positively or negatively, and a phenomenon known as the framing effect is responsible for this.

Much research has been devoted to identifying loss aversion tendencies in the housing market. Genesove and Mayer (2001) noted that Boston housing sellers are loss-averse because of falling market prices, indicating a positive correlation between housing prices and housing transaction volumes. Similarly, Anenberg (2011), studying the housing market in the San Francisco Bay Area, highlighted that sellers, when faced with nominal losses from their housing investments, significantly increased the prices at which they would be willing to sell their properties. However, Bao and Meng (2017) emphasise that despite great progress in identifying loss aversion in the housing market, there is still much work to be done in this area, particularly in terms of reliably measuring loss and properly identifying reference points. One consequence of loss aversion is the endowment effect which has important implications for the housing market (Gibb, 2009). Therefore, this effect is the focus of this study.

Purpose of the monograph

In the housing market, the endowment effect can lead to deviations in selling and buying property prices from the market prices. Specifically, this cognitive bias results in the minimum prices that sellers would be willing to accept (WTA) to sell residential properties being lower than the maximum prices that buyers would be willing to pay for them (WTP). This leads to friction between the demand and supply sides of the housing market, contributing to an imbalance and a reduction in the number of transactions. To date, empirical studies have mostly looked at the endowment effect for simple goods such as mugs or pens. The first empirical study to identify the endowment effect for housing goods emerged only in 2014. In the following years, more work has been produced, both theoretically and empirically, to increase the understanding of how this phenomenon operates in the housing market. However, there is a lack of literature that synthesises the achievements of researchers in terms of the endowment effect in the housing market. Theoretical and empirical considerations of endowment effects in different segments of the housing market are also absent. Consequently, the aim of this monograph is threefold.

A1) to provide an overview of the research on the endowment effect in the housing market.

A2) to develop a theoretical model explaining the magnitude of endowment effects in the sales and rental housing markets, with a distinction between primary and secondary markets.

A3) to assess the presence of endowment effects in Poland's sales and rental housing markets.

Chapter overviews

Chapter 1 provides an overview of the existing theoretical and empirical works on the endowment effect in the housing market using the systematic literature review method, and pursues objective A1. The review is preceded by a presentation of the essence of the endowment effect as well as its genesis to introduce the reader to the issue of behavioural bias under analysis. The literature review revealed that the identification of the endowment effect in the housing market has, so far, been a problem rarely addressed by researchers. To date, only ten empirical studies have been conducted. The results across publications proved to be consistent; that is, the endowment effect is present in the housing market, but its strength is moderated by various factors, including, among others, the property market cycle and respondent characteristics. The literature review has highlighted several research gaps. For example, behavioural researchers should (i) seek alternative explanations for the overvaluation of goods by their owners to obtain reliable estimates of the endowment effect, (ii) develop a theory of multiple reference points, and (iii) attempt to identify endowment effects for different segments of the housing market. In summary, this chapter answers the following research questions.

RQ1. Has the endowment effect been identified in existing housing studies? If so, which factors moderate the strength of the endowment effect?

RQ2. What are the challenges in measuring the endowment effect on housing goods?

RQ3. What are the research gaps in identifying the endowment effect in the housing market?

Chapter 2 pursues objective A2 and, therefore, aims to develop a theoretical model to explain the strength of the endowment effect in sales and rental housing markets, with a distinction between primary and secondary markets. This part of the monograph responds to some of the identified research gaps in Chapter 1. The discussion on the size of the endowment effect is preceded by a description of the basics of the housing market to understand its functioning. The theoretical model presented suggests that sellers/landlords and buyers/tenants, when estimating the price/rent of a residential property, consider the nature of the transacted good (exchangeable/consumable) and have multiple reference points. It is postulated that the endowment effect will be lowered in primary markets (sales and rental) where sellers/landlords treat housing as goods for sale/rent, and therefore, they do not demand additional compensation for the loss of property ownership and/or possession. However, in this case, sellers/landlords can adjust their property self-valuations depending on the reference prices. The strongest endowment effect is likely to occur in the secondary sales market, where sellers use dwellings for consumption purposes. In turn, in the secondary rental market, the endowment effect is predicted to occur but will be weaker than in the sales market, as the landlord making the transaction only compensates for the loss of possession over the property, rather than possession and legal ownership. In summary, this chapter answers the following research questions.

RQ4. From a theoretical perspective, what are the reference points in housing transactions and how do they affect the formation of the endowment effect in the housing market?

RQ5. According to the theory, does the strength of endowment effects differ between sales and rental housing markets and across primary and secondary markets?

Chapter 3 pursues objective A3 and, in particular, aims to assess the presence of endowment effects in the sales and rental housing markets in Poland, taking into account the theoretical predictions conceptualised in Chapter 2. The chapter begins with a presentation of the specifics of the Polish housing market, including data on (i) price levels, (ii) the size of sales and rental markets distinguishing between primary and secondary markets, and (iii) housing affordability. This study intends to provide the reader with the context of the Polish housing market against other markets. A lab-in-the-field experiment was used to obtain data, and the contingent valuation method (CVM) was employed to elicit WTA and WTP values. Groups of Polish homeowners and renters participated in the experiment, with divisions into sellers/landlords and buyers/tenants. The findings suggest that the endowment effect significantly shapes the housing market in Poland, with its strength varying across segments. In summary, this chapter answers the following research questions.

RQ6. Is there an endowment effect on the Polish housing market? If so, does the magnitude of the endowment effect differ between sales and rental markets, and across primary and secondary markets?

Contribution

This book contributes to the current economic literature in several ways. First, a systematic review of the literature indicates the problems and future research directions in identifying the endowment effect in the housing market. Second, it provides a theoretical explanation for the strength of the endowment effect in different segments of the housing market, considering the concept of multiple reference points. In particular, the primary and secondary residential sales and rental markets were analysed. Third, this monograph presents the first empirical research results to date on the strength of the endowment effect in the Polish housing market, broken down into various segments.

This book is important to politicians, researchers, and students. Thanks to this book, it will be possible to identify those segments of the housing market which, due to their elevated endowment effects, should be the subject of government intervention, as well as those whose development should be encouraged due to their low friction resulting from the reduced magnitude of the cognitive bias under study. In turn, for behavioural scientists, this monograph organises knowledge on the endowment effect in the housing market, provides new empirical evidence for its existence, and indicates several new research directions in the field. Ultimately, researchers using this book can teach students both the theoretical and practical aspects of the endowment effect using the case study presented in Chapter 3.

References

Anenberg, E. (2011). Loss aversion, equity constraints and seller behavior in the real estate market. *Regional Science and Urban Economics*, *41*(1), 67–76. https://doi.org/10.1016/j.regsciurbeco.2010.08.003

Baddeley, M. (2019). *Behavioural economics and finance*. Routledge.

Bao, H. X., & Meng, C. C. (2017). Loss aversion and housing studies. *Journal of Real Estate Literature*, *25*(1), 49–75. https://doi.org/10.1080/10835547.2017.12090454

Boelhouwer, P. (2011). Neo-classical economic theory on housing markets and behavioural sciences: Ally or opponent? *Housing, Theory and Society*, *28*(3), 276–280. https://doi.org/10.1080/14036096.2011.599173

Camerer, C. F. (1999). Behavioral economics: Reunifying psychology and economics. *Proceedings of the National Academy of Sciences*, *96*(19), 10575–10577. https://doi.org/10.1073/pnas.96.19.10575

Camerer, C. F., & Loewenstein, G. (2004). Behavioral economics: Past, present and future. In C. F. Camerer, G. Loewenstein, & M. Rabin (Eds.), *Advances in behavioral economics* (pp. 3–51). Princeton University Press.

Cascão, A., Quelhas, A. P., & Cunha, A. M. (2023). Heuristics and cognitive biases in the housing investment market. *International Journal of Housing Markets and Analysis*, *16*(5), 991–1006. https://doi.org/10.1108/IJHMA-05-2022-0073

Dale, S. (2015). Heuristics and biases: The science of decision-making. *Business Information Review*, *32*(2), 93–99. https://doi.org/10.1177/0266382115592536

Dunning, R. J. (2017). Competing notions of search for home: Behavioural economics and housing markets. *Housing, Theory and Society*, *34*(1), 21–37. https://doi.org/10.1080/14036096.2016.1190784

Earl, P. E. (2005). *Behavioral economics and the economics of regulation*. School of Economics, The University of Queensland.

Earl, P. E. (2018). Richard H. Thaler: A nobel prize for behavioural economics. *Review of Political Economy*, *30*(2), 107–125. https://doi.org/10.1080/09538259.2018.1513236

Earl, P. E., & Littleboy, B. (2014). *G. L. S. Shackle*. Palgrave Macmillan.

Folmer, H. (2009). Why sociology is better conditioned to explain economic behaviour than economics. *Kyklos*, *62*(2), 258–274. https://doi.org/10.1111/j.1467-6435.2009.00435.x

Genesove, D., & Mayer, C. (2001). Loss aversion and seller behavior: Evidence from the housing market. *The Quarterly Journal of Economics*, *116*(4), 1233–1260. https://doi.org/10.1162/003355301753265561

Gibb, K. (2009). Housing studies and the role of economic theory: An (applied) disciplinary perspective. *Housing, Theory and Society*, *26*(1), 26–40. https://doi.org/10.1080/14036090802704262

Ho, T. H., Lim, N., & Camerer, C. F. (2006). Modeling the psychology of consumer and firm behavior with behavioral economics. *Journal of Marketing Research*, *43*(3), 307–331. https://doi.org/10.1509/jmkr.43.3.307

Horenstein, A. R., Osgood, D., & Snir, A. (2017). Out-of-town buyers, mispricing and the availability heuristic in a housing market. *Real Estate Finance*, *34*(1), 27–35.

Hosseini, H. (2011). George Katona: A founding father of old behavioral economics. *The Journal of Socio-Economics*, *40*(6), 977–984. https://doi.org/10.1016/j.socec.2011.04.002

Kahneman, D. (2003). Maps of bounded rationality: Psychology for behavioral economics. *American Economic Review*, *93*(5), 1449–1475. https://doi.org/10.1257/000282803322655392

Kahneman, D., & Tversky, A. (1979). Prospect theory: An analysis of decision under risk. *Econometrica*, *47*(2), 263–292. https://doi.org/10.2307/1914185

Katona, G. (1975). *Psychological economics*. Elsevier.

Kokot, S. (2023). The effect of price anchoring on the housing market based on studies of local markets in Poland. *Real Estate Management and Valuation, 31*(3), 44–57. https://doi.org/10.2478/remav-2023-0020

Leung, T. C. (2004). Macroeconomics and housing: A review of the literature. *Journal of Housing Economics, 13*(4), 249–267. https://doi.org/10.1016/j.jhe.2004.09.002

Leung, T. C., & Tsang, K. P. (2013). Anchoring and loss aversion in the housing market: Implications on price dynamics. *China Economic Review, 24*, 42–54. https://doi.org/10.1016/j.chieco.2012.10.003

Levy, D. S., Frethey-Bentham, C., & Cheung, W. K. S. (2020). Asymmetric framing effects and market familiarity: Experimental evidence from the real estate market. *Journal of Property Research, 37*(1), 85–104. https://doi.org/10.1080/09599916.2020.1713858

Malik, M. A. S., Zafar, M., Ullah, S., & Ullah, A. (2021). Role of behavioral biases in real estate prices in Pakistan. *Real Estate Management and Valuation, 29*(1), 41–53. https://doi.org/10.2478/remav-2021-0005

Mallard, G. (2016). *Bounded rationality and behavioural economics*. Routledge.

Marschak, J. (1950). Rational behavior, uncertain prospects, and measurable utility. *Econometrica, 18*(2), 111–141. https://doi.org/10.2307/1907264

Marsh, A., & Gibb, K. (2011). Uncertainty, expectations and behavioural aspects of housing market choices. *Housing, Theory and Society, 28*(3), 215–235. https://doi.org/10.1080/14036096.2011.599182

Neszveda, G. (2018). The contribution of thaler to behavioural economics. *Financial and Economic Review, 17*(1), 153–167. https://doi.org/10.25201/FER.17.1.153167

Rosen, S. (1974). Hedonic prices and implicit markets: Product differentiation in pure competition. *Journal of Political Economy, 82*(1), 34–55. https://doi.org/10.1086/260169

Sent, E. M. (2004). Behavioral economics: How psychology made its (limited) way back into economics. *History of Political Economy, 36*(4), 735–760. https://doi.org/10.1215/00182702-36-4-735

Simon, H. (1957). *Models of man*. Wiley.

Smith, S. J. (2011). Home price dynamics: A behavioural economy? *Housing, Theory and Society, 28*(3), 236–261. https://doi.org/10.1080/14036096.2011.599179

Thaler, R. (1980). Toward a positive theory of consumer choice. *Journal of Economic Behavior & Organization, 1*(1), 39–60. https://doi.org/10.1016/0167-2681(80)90051-7

Tomal, M., & Brzezicka, J. (2023). Certainty equivalent, risk attitudes and housing. *Applied Economics Letters, 30*(18), 2576–2580. https://doi.org/10.1080/13504851.2022.2099797

Tversky, A., & Kahneman, D. (1974). Judgment under uncertainty: Heuristics and biases. *Science, 185*(4157), 1124–1131. https://doi. org/10.1126/science.185.4157.1124

Wilkinson, N., & Klaes, M. (2017). *An introduction to behavioral economics*. Bloomsbury Publishing.

1 The endowment effect and housing studies

A review

Chapter overview

This chapter provides an overview of research on the endowment effect in the housing market using a systematic literature review method. The review is followed by an indication of the essence of the endowment effect and its causes, mainly according to the behavioural school, but also according to the neoclassical and institutional approaches. To date, the endowment effect literature has tended to focus on simple items, such as cups or pens. In the context of housing goods, research on the endowment effect started after 2000 and has been conducted in two of its paradigms, that is, the exchange and valuation paradigms, with more research produced under the latter. In general, the results of research on the endowment effect in the housing market are consistent; that is, this cognitive bias is present, but its strength varies according to different factors. For example, the endowment effect may differ between housing market cycles and social groups. This review indicates that there are still many research gaps in this topic. In summary, this chapter answers the following research questions.

RQ1. Has the endowment effect been identified in existing housing studies? If so, which factors moderate the strength of the endowment effect?

RQ2. What are the challenges in measuring the endowment effect on housing goods?

RQ3. What are the research gaps in identifying the endowment effect in the housing market?

DOI: 10.1201/9781003512004-2

1.1   The essence of the endowment effect

1.1.1   The endowment effect definition

The endowment effect is defined as the tendency to overvalue owned goods. This effect was first conceptualised by Thaler (1980) and has become one of the best empirically proven behavioural biases (Loewenstein & Issacharoff, 1994). Morewedge and Giblin (2015) point out that the endowment effect occurs in two experimental paradigms: the exchange and valuation paradigms.

Under the exchange paradigm, people are less likely to exchange a good in its endowment for other goods (Knetsch, 1989). Such behaviour violates standard economic theory, in which endowment should not matter, and the proportion of preferred goods should be similar. In the presence of the endowment effect, the indifference curves are not completely reversible, and the rate of commodity substitution depends on whether good A is exchanged for B or vice versa.[1] People's higher preference for resources in their endowment creates friction in markets for goods as well as economic entitlements (Kahneman et al., 1990).

In contrast, under the valuation paradigm, the minimum prices at which sellers are willing to accept (WTA) selling goods is higher than the maximum prices at which buyers are willing to pay (WTP) to obtain them, leading to a WTA-WTP gap. Previous research indicates that this gap varies depending on the nature of the goods. Horowitz and McConnell (2002) indicated that the WTA-WTP gap is low for ordinary private items and significantly higher for non-market public goods. Moreover, the endowment effect is generally attributed to consumer goods as opposed to exchange goods (Kahneman, 1992). The literature also demonstrates that the endowment effect decreases when the trading parties' market experience increases. List (2003) reveals that the WTA-WTP gap disappears for traders who perform more than six transactions per month and have many years of experience. Similarly, List (2004), using a naturally occurring market, found a negative correlation between the intensity of the market experience and the WTA-WTP gap. According to Engelmann and Hollard (2010), the reduced strength of the endowment effect in more experienced traders is because market experience contributes to the elimination of uncertainty associated with the transaction.

The occurrence of the WTA-WTP gap violates the rational choice theory, claiming that people are reference-independent when valuing goods (Tversky & Kahneman, 1991). The WTA-WTP gap is also not in line with the Coase theorem, which assumes that the allocation of goods is independent of the initially assigned rights to objects in the absence of wealth effects and transaction costs (Ericson & Fuster, 2014). In this context, Kahneman et al. (1990) conducted a series of bilateral bargaining experiments on consumer goods, such as cups, and found that contrary to what the Coase theorem predicts, the volume of transactions is much lower because of the endowment effect. Similar conclusions were also reached by Jacques (1992), who concluded that, in real-life situations, the Coase theorem does not hold because of the presence of the endowment effect. The imbalance between WTA and WTP leads to a significant reduction in the number of transactions in markets compared with standard economic theory and legal analysis predictions. This hinders policymakers' efforts in terms of policies and laws aimed at allocating and distributing goods in society (More-wedge & Giblin, 2015). In this regard, Hovenkamp (1991) noted that the endowment effect undermines the validity of welfare economics and results in total social wealth being maximised only when entitlements are allocated initially to those who value them the most; in other words, to the individual who has the highest WTA.[2]

1.1.2   The origins of the WTA-WTP gap

Two approaches to explain the WTA-WTP gap can be found in the literature.[3] The first, a broad one, assumes that the endowment effect means the WTA-WTP gap, regardless of the genesis of its origin (Morewedge & Giblin, 2015). The second, a narrow one, assumes that the endowment effect is only a part of the WTA-WTP gap, which results from loss aversion and its determinants (Brown, 2005). The following are the most important sources of the WTA-WTP gap.

Loss aversion

This tendency is a traditional determinant of the endowment effect and is based on Kahneman and Tversky's (1979) prospect theory. The latter assumes that buyers and sellers frame their decisions as either gains or losses, depending on a reference point, which is most often taken as the status quo. For sellers, the reference point is "owning" the good and the selling process sets its reference point to not owning. For buyers, the opposite occurs: the transaction shifts the reference point from not owning the good to owning it. Under prospect theory, the value function is steeper in the loss domain than in the gain domain, causing people to experience losses more strongly than equivalent gains (see Figure 1.1) (Tversky & Kahneman, 1992). Consequently, the seller, to compensate for his/her loss, increases the WTA value, resulting in a WTA-WTP gap.

The literature has proven that loss aversion depends on several psychological factors. For example, Ariely et al. (2005) mentioned the constructs of emotional attachment and cognitive perspective. Emotional attachment assumes that the reluctance to give up a good rises as consumers' attachment to the good increases, resulting in a higher valuation of the good. In the literature, it is expected that emotional attachment can cause an initial endowment effect due to typical people's responses with respect to possession. In addition, Strahilevitz and Loewenstein (1998) argue that, with the length of ownership, emotional attachment leads to an intensification of the endowment effect. The cognitive perspective, on the other hand, is based on analysing

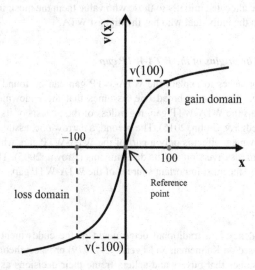

Figure 1.1 Value function under prospect theory.

Source: Adapted from Kahneman and Tversky (1979).

Note: Losses looms more than gains, i.e. $|v(-100)| > v(100)$.

differences in perceptions of buying and selling tasks and examining how these differences affect information processing. Carmon and Ariely (2000) specify that sellers focus on sentiment toward surrendering the good, which causes selling prices to be influenced by factors such as the benefits of owning it. Buyers, on the other hand, tend to analyse sentiment toward what they forgo (i.e. expenditure), so buying prices are influenced by reference prices. In this case, sellers tend to price goods higher than buyers which creates a WTA-WTP gap. However, when a seller's goal is to sell a product to gain income (the differential perspective account), they may focus on what they can gain rather than lose, which should lead to the vanishing of the endowment effect. Novemsky and Kahneman (2005) similarly argue that exchange goods are given away intentionally and therefore this type of transaction is not judged as a loss. On the other hand, van Dijk and van Knippenberg (1996) demonstrated that the endowment effect can occur for these types of goods only when traders are uncertain about future exchange prices. In this case, loss aversion results from the difficulty in calculating net gains and losses when exchange rates are uncertain.

Mandel (2002) also highlighted the problem of agents' attitudes toward a potential transaction and suggested that the strength of the endowment effect may depend on transaction demand,[4] that is, the motivation of buyers and sellers toward the transaction. When sellers have a high need for a transaction, they may be more willing to lower selling prices. Similarly, when buyers want a good, they may be willing to increase the prices proposed for it. When both parties are simultaneously characterised by high transaction demand, the endowment effect may disappear or even reverse. In addition, Mandel (2002) notes that transaction demand tends to be high for exchange goods and low for consumer goods. However, for goods intended for use, the endowment effect can also be reduced because of low user satisfaction with these goods. Mandel (2002) also pointed out that transaction demand can change the reference point. For example, people with high transaction demands may view a failed transaction as a loss.

Shu and Peck (2011) proposed that the mechanism of emotional attachment can be divided into two separate constructs: psychological ownership and affective reaction. The first measures whether a loss is perceived, while the second measures the intensity of that loss. According to the Pierce et al. (2003) model, psychological ownership is induced through one of the following mechanisms: possession of the good (exercising control over it), actual or imagined use (becoming familiar with it), and identification with the good (investing self in the good). Therefore, non-legal owners may experience psychological ownership. On the other hand, Shu and Peck (2011) emphasise that legal ownership can occur without psychological ownership in situations where the good is not part of the endowment, as a result of changes in the cognitive perspective. In such situations, surrendering the object is not considered a loss because the reference point is "not owning". In this vein, Reb and Connolly (2007) proved that the endowment effect is triggered mainly by exercising control over an object, whereby a subjective sense of endowment is created. Reb and Connolly (2007) argue that in the no-possession situation, giving away the object is treated more as foregone gain. By contrast, according to the construct's assumptions of affective reaction, higher levels of emotion or affect have a strong effect on loss aversion. Shu and Peck (2011) indicated that the perceived magnitude of the loss may increase as a result of strong affective reactions derived from general mood and positive and negative emotions related to the object or its nature (Brenner et al., 2007).

Chatterjee et al. (2013), in order to explain the endowment effect, emphasised that owning a good is a reference point for both loss aversion and the relationship between the person and the object (the ownership account). According to the researchers, the linking of these two drivers of the endowment effect leads to a construct called self-threat, which results in a self-enhancing valuation of the good. In this case, the endowment effect is the effect of self-threat produced by the potential loss of the good with which we associate. Notably, Chatterjee et al. (2013) treat the ownership account independently of loss aversion rather than as a moderator. Morewedge and Giblin (2015) propose that the ownership account can also manifest through a self-referential memory effect. This relies on the fact that during transactions, owners usually spontaneously recall the very positive attributes of a given good, which should increase their valuation of that good. However, when the goods in question are associated with only negative attributes, a reversal of the endowment effect can occur.

Researchers have also focused on the reference-point issue when explaining the endowment effect based on loss aversion. For example, Weaver and Frederick (2012) developed the reference price theory. According to this theory, sellers' prices are elevated because the reference prices at which consumers assess transactions exceed their internal valuations. This theory assumes that the reference point during a transaction is a good reference price rather than the ownership of the item.

Knetsch and Wong (2009) highlight the role of manipulating the strength of the reference point in the context of creating an endowment effect. They found evidence that when the reference point was weak, that is, the initial assignment of goods to participants in the experiment occurred randomly, they had no physical possession over them, and the final questions in the experiment were framed in neutral terms, the endowment effect within the exchange paradigm did not arise. The opposite occurs when the manipulation of the experiment strengthens the reference point. Knetsch and Wong (2009) designed this enhancement in three ways: (i) allowing participants in the experiment to physically control the goods, (ii) emphasising that the initial assignment of goods was not random, and (iii) framing the questions deliberately in terms of losses and gains. It is important to note that the results of Knetsch and Wong (2009) are in line with those obtained by Reb and Connolly (2007), in the sense that both of these analyses highlight the fact that possession rather than ownership is crucial for the endowment effect to appear.

Tversky and Kahneman (1991) and Kahneman (1992) emphasised that when people make decisions, they have multiple reference points in terms of which transaction can be viewed as a gain or loss (e.g. aspirations, expectations, norms, or social comparisons). Ericson and Fuster (2014) note that there is currently no empirical evidence of the relative validity of different reference points for riskless decisions. Kőszegi and Rabin (2006) and Ericson and Fuster (2014) assumed that the reference point is not the status quo but rather a reference point based on expectations, i.e. a person's probabilistic beliefs about the outcome of a transaction. In this case, when the seller is certain of the occurrence of the transaction, his/her reference point becomes the state of not owning the good, so the transaction itself is not evaluated as a loss, resulting in a lack of an endowment effect. On the other hand, a buyer who evaluates the transaction as certain but fails to complete it will be inclined to increase the WTP value, as he/she will treat such a situation as a loss (Rosato, 2016). It should be noted that the Kőszegi and Rabin (2006) model,[5] in contrast to the Tversky and Kahneman (1991) model, assumes that the reference point is stochastic and allows the identification of the endowment effect under risk. For choices under uncertainty, Sprenger (2015) postulated the use of multiple reference points.

Neoclassical explanations

Mainstream economists often attribute the WTA-WTP gap to the income effect (Willig, 1976). The latter occurs when the payment for obtaining a good is constrained by income and, on the other hand, the compensation for giving it away is not. In particular, the WTA can exceed WTP when the income elasticity of demand is so large that income limits the ability to pay (Brown & Gregory, 1999). The income effect size depends on prices and the availability of substitutes, that is, for a given good, WTA will not be higher than the price of a perfect substitute. Consequently, the fewer substitutes a good has, the higher the WTA-WTP gap (Hanemann, 1991). On this basis, Brown and Gregory (1999) suggest that the gap between WTA and WTP should be small for inexpensive items and larger for unique and valuable goods.

New institutional economics

New institutional economics (NIE) analyses institutions and their relationships with organisational arrangements. Institutions can be defined as the rules, norms, and constraints created by people to reduce uncertainty. NIE rejects the assumption of mainstream economics that people are fully informed and rational during decision-making (Menard & Shirley, 2005). Instead, NIE accepts the concept of bounded rationality (Dequech, 2006), as in old behavioural economics. Economists within NIE emphasise that transactions involve the costs necessary to acquire information to reduce uncertainty about future events. In this context, Brown (2005) points out that the WTA-WTP gap may be growing because sellers may increase the selling price due to the potential transaction costs associated with buying another good that is a substitute for the good being sold. Further, sellers and buyers can try to cover the costs of carrying out the transaction, such as taxes, by increasing the WTA and decreasing the WTP.

Strategic motives

Brown (2005) suggests that the WTA-WTP gap may be the result of both the seller and buyer's focus on getting a good deal during negotiations. In this case, the seller has a strategic tendency to set the highest possible price that a potential buyer can pay. Conversely, the buyer tends to set a lower price. However, Kurt and Inman (2013) proved that both sellers and buyers do not predict the endowment effect, so it is not presumed in advance by transaction parties. Furthermore, Knutson et al. (2008) argue that the WTA-WTP gap occurs even when people are given one chance to complete a transaction. Finally, Morewedge and Giblin (2015) concluded that in many studies that attribute the endowment effect to strategic motives, the experimental procedure itself has a significant influence on the results.

Evolutionary approach

Huck et al. (2005) proposed that the tendency to overvalue goods is a result of human evolution as it provides an advantage during negotiations. According to this approach, people who overvalued their possessions acquired more resources through trade, enabling them to support more offspring. The predisposition to overvaluing possessions is inadvertently and incorrectly extended to incentive-compatible market situations, in which the best interest is to reveal how goods are really valued.

Other

Brown (2005) and Brown and Gregory (1999) pointed to several other economic and psychological factors causing the WTA-WTP gap. They categorised implied value as an economic factor and legitimacy, ambiguity, and responsibility as psychological factors. The implied value mechanism assumes that during a transaction, a signal is sent: the good offered for sale may be unwanted for the seller which reduces its value, whereas for the buyer, the good may be perceived as desirable which increases its valuation. Legitimacy refers to considering the ethical dimensions of specific transactions, especially in the context of health and safety. In this case, the WTA may increase as a result of social norms opposing giving away health or safety for money. Ambiguity concerns risk-averse buyers and sellers who, due to insufficient information, may lower WTP or overvalue WTA, respectively, to avoid making a decision they might regret in the future. Ambiguity is consistent with the concept of the impact of information asymmetry (derived from new Keynesian economics) on the WTA-WTP gap. In this case, buyers reduce the WTP value to compensate for the uncertainty and risks associated with the transaction. Responsibility refers to the mechanism of feeling morally responsible for goods entrusted to a person. WTA is increased because when the possible effect of a transaction is harmful, then the preferred action is the status quo: people feel less bad if the harm is not caused by their actions. Therefore, to avoid actions that may cause harm, WTA is inflated, and WTP is understated.

1.1.3   Measurement of the WTA-WTP gap

In the valuation paradigm of the endowment effect, the WTA-WTP gap de facto indicates a statistically significant difference between the mean/median WTA of all potential sellers and mean/median WTP of all potential buyers. Identifying the WTA-WTP gap in practice requires the following steps: 1) eliciting the WTA and WTP values; 2) calculating the mean/median WTA and WTP values; and 3) comparing the WTA and WTP average values using statistical tests or econometric methods.

To calculate the average WTA and WTP values, data on the entire distribution is necessary. Unfortunately, the WTA and WTP values are not directly observable and cannot be replaced by market data. This is because the latter data reflect only part of the WTA and WTP distributions, that is, where the WTA distribution overlaps with the WTP distribution. Therefore, using market data such as housing transaction prices will lead to biased average WTA and WTP values (Bao, 2020). Therefore, in previous studies on the endowment effect, the WTA and WTP values were generated artificially using stated preference methods. One of the most popular is the contingent valuation method (CVM), in which individuals are asked about the maximum price they would be willing to pay (WTP) or the minimum price they would be willing to accept (WTA) to make a deal (MacDonald & Bowker, 1994). In this case, the question is most often asked in an open-ended manner; therefore, the average values of WTA and WTP may be subject to extreme responses and distortions if respondents treat the question as a prelude to negotiation (Reb & Connolly, 2007). Bao (2020) also stresses that the problem of eliciting WTA and WTP may be particularly related to public goods, which first do not have a market, and secondly may produce non-honest answers. CVM is often used in laboratory, field, natural, and lab-in-the-field experiments or different types of surveys.

The BDM auction developed by Becker et al. (1964) is also popular in measuring the endowment effect using the WTA-WTP gap. This method involves asking participants in a secret experiment about their WTP and WTA by marking a price from the available prices on a prepared workbook. One price from the workbook is then drawn at random and made available to the experiment participants, after which buyers and sellers have the opportunity to sell or buy the product at the drawn price. This procedure is repeated several times, so the experiment participants have the opportunity to adjust their WTA and WTP. The use of a randomised exchange price in the BDM auction is designed to avoid respondents feeling that it can influence the exchange price. The Vickrey auction (1961), which assumes that the bidder's dominant strategy is to announce their true WTP and WTA, is also used to identify the endowment effect. The Vickrey auction for WTP highlights that announcing an excessively elevated WTP will result in paying too high a price for the good, whereas announcing too low a WTP will increase the chances of not winning the auction. In this auction, participants are asked to provide their WTP or WTA for an item in an open-ended question without using price intervals, after which the second-highest WTP value and the second-lowest WTA value are revealed. Shogren et al. (2001) suggested that the endowment effect can be eliminated by successive iterations of the Vickrey auction.

1.2 Literature review

1.2.1 The method

This review on the incidence of the endowment effect in the housing market uses the systematic literature review method. The primary advantage of this method is that it identifies all relevant research within the set research questions; therefore, the summary of the literature is unbiased (Nightingale, 2009). A systematic literature review consists of the following elements (Egger & Smith, 2001): (i) formulation of the research questions; (ii) definition of the inclusion and exclusion criteria of the studies from the review; (iii) location of the studies; (iv) selection of the studies; (v) assessment of the quality of the studies; (vi) extraction of data from the studies; and (vii) analysis, presentation, and interpretation of the results.

Research questions

This review aimed to answer the following research question: RQ1. Has the endowment effect been identified in existing housing studies?

If so, which factors moderate the strength of the endowment effect?; RQ2. What are the challenges in measuring the endowment effect on housing goods?; RQ3. What are the research gaps in identifying the endowment effect in the housing market?

Inclusion and exclusion criteria

The primary inclusion criterion was the subject matter of the research undertaken; that is, it must relate to the endowment effect and housing, and this could represent theoretical considerations as well as empirical evidence. The publication period was not narrowed. The exclusion criteria included the lack of a compatible research topic, as well as retracted publications, encyclopaedic publications, and editorials.

Locating and selecting studies with quality assessment

The SCOPUS and Web of Science databases were used to identify scientific publications investigating the endowment effect in the housing market using the following query: ("endowment effect" OR "endowment effects" OR "WTA/WTP" OR "WTA–WTP" OR "WTA-WTP") AND (housing OR house OR "real estate" OR dwelling). A list of 65 publications was obtained, of which, 23 duplicate records were removed. Sixty-four publications came from the SCOPUS and Web of Science, and one was added from the Google Books catalogue after checking for potential book positions. This was followed by a preliminary analysis of the list of publications, which resulted in the elimination of two encyclopaedic records (reason 1), one retracted publication (reason 2), one editorial (reason 3), and 22 publications whose content was not relevant to this review (reason 4). After a detailed examination of the remaining publications, a further four items were removed from the list, among which: (i) three did not study the endowment effect (reason 5) but only justified the results obtained with it, and (ii) one was about the financial market (reason 6). Subsequently, the quality of the included studies was assessed. First, the empirical papers were analysed, namely, the compatibility of their conceptual assumptions with the endowment effect theory. On this basis, we decided to remove one publication that had questionable research underpinnings (reason 7); in particular, potential property buyers were asked questions intended for sellers. The final list of studies used in the review includes 11 publications (see Figure 1.2) of which ten are empirical and one is purely theoretical.

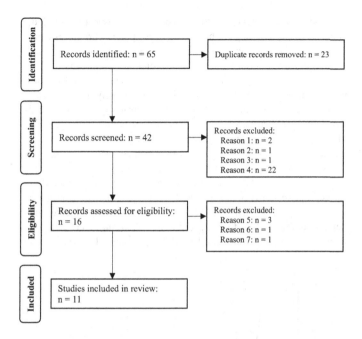

Figure 1.2 PRISMA flow diagram.

Source: Adapted from Page et al. (2021).

Data extraction and analysis

In the publications reviewed, attention is focused on issues that will enable the research questions to be answered, in particular, the strength of the endowment effect in the housing markets studied, the factors that alter its intensity, and the problems associated with its measurement. Finally, this review identified research gaps in the topic under study.

1.2.2 Main findings from endowment effect studies: the exchange paradigm

Previous studies have analysed the occurrence of the endowment effect in two paradigms. In the exchange paradigm, the problem of residential mobility in society has been studied. Morrison and Clark (2016) and

Yan and Bao (2018) suggest that, according to prospect theory, individuals should generally not be willing to swap their current residence for another. This is because people take their current home, which is their legal ownership or possession, as a reference point. Additionally, people become attached to their neighbourhoods and general locations, which can also serve as reference points. Ultimately, people's decisions to move from one place to another are strongly directed towards the status quo; that is, staying in their current home. In the presence of the endowment effect, the indifference curves are irreversible, and the initial allocation of households to given locations influences their decisions regarding residential mobility (see Figure 1.3).

Morrison and Clark (2016) highlight that the endowment effect creates a gap between the use and exchange value of a property, with owners being tied to the former. Ultimately, to relocate, they demand compensation to mitigate the loss resulting from giving up their current homes. Clark and Lisowski (2017) conclude that among

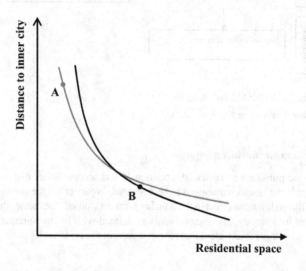

Figure 1.3 Irreversible indifference curves for two goods: distance to the inner city and residential space.

Source: Adapted from Morrison and Clark (2016), Ericson and Fuster (2014) and Alonso (1960).

Note: Location A is preferred to B when starting from A and location B is preferred to A when starting from B.

speculators or traders in the housing market, the endowment effect does not occur because, in their case, use value plays no role. The issue of the use and exchange values of property in the context of the existence of endowment effects was also addressed by Cheung et al. (2023), who found that the greater the exchangeable nature of a housing good, the greater the number of transactions in the housing market.

The empirical results support the aforementioned theoretical assumptions (see Table 1.1). Clark and Lisowski (2017) investigated

Table 1.1 Empirical research on the endowment effect – the exchange paradigm.

Author	Methods	Results
Clark and Lisowski (2017)	Longitudinal survey in Australia in 2010–2014 (N=7,091). Endowment effects are defined explicitly as: (1) households owning a dwelling; or (2) time living at one address for more than 5 years; or (3) socioeconomic quality of the neighbourhood.	Households with home ownership are less likely to move compared to renters. In addition, a longer period of residence at one address reduces the likelihood of moving.
Yan and Bao (2018)	Natural experiment in China in 2016 (N=253). The endowment effect is defined explicitly as attachment to a former place of residence.	People express greater satisfaction with forced relocation if they return to or near their previous place of residence.
Cheung et al. (2023)	Quasi-experiment in China based on transaction data in 2011–2015 (N=12,650). The weakening of the endowment effect is adopted as an increase in the number of transactions in the market.	An increase in the number of transactions has been noticed in the government-shared housing market following the implementation of the WFB policy due to the increased exchangeable nature of this type of housing.

Source: Own study.

whether endowment effects can influence a household's decision to change its residence. This study assumed that the endowment effect is characterised by households with legal ownership of the dwelling as well as those with a long history of living at one address. The socio-economic status of the neighbourhood was taken as the last variable, proxying the endowment effect. The results revealed that owners move less frequently than renters do. In addition, households with longer residence times at one address were less likely to change their residences. Using a natural experiment in China, Yan and Bao (2018) investigated whether the endowment effect affected people's satisfaction with forcible relocation. This study assumed that the endowment effect takes the form of attachment to the former place of residence. The results indicated that people expressed greater satisfaction with forced relocation if they returned to or near their former housing location. Finally, Cheung et al. (2023) demonstrated that dwellings that have an exchangeable nature in addition to a consumption nature are more likely to be traded on the market. The authors performed a quasi-experiment in Hong Kong and assumed that the larger the government's share in the ownership of a dwelling, the greater its exchangeable nature owing to the introduction of the White Form Buyer (WFB) policy, which allows owner-occupiers to sell their flats without repaying the government's share. A larger value of the latter reduces the value of the compensation for selling the dwelling, as its purchase price is reduced by the size of this share.

1.2.3   Main findings from endowment effect studies: the valuation paradigm

Considerations of the endowment effect from the point of view of the valuation paradigm have received considerable attention from researchers to date (see Table 1.2). These works aimed to assess whether there is a WTA-WTP gap for housing goods, which distinguishes them from studies based on the exchange paradigm, where the endowment effect was directly approximated by selected variables or adopted as a change in the number of transactions in the market.

He and Asami (2014) were the first to analyse the endowment effect for housing goods in the context of land expropriation issues in China.[6] The authors collected data using a field survey, and the measurement of WTA and WTP was performed using a dichotomous choice method. Respondents were asked about the price of buying another house with cash obtained through compensation (WTP) and the price they would

Table 1.2 Empirical research on the endowment effect – the valuation paradigm.

Author	Methods	Results
Nash and Rosenthal (2014)	Natural experiment in the USA (N=265). The endowment effect was defined as the WTA-WTP gap in a broad manner. The CVM method, specifically an open-ended question, was used to elicit WTA and WTP.	The mean WTA value was 5.74 and the mean WTP value was 2.79, translating into a WTA-WTP gap of 2.05. The WTA-WTP gap widened several months after the survey was repeated.
He and Asami (2014)	Field survey in China in 2010–2011 (N=630). The endowment effect is defined as the WTA-WTP gap in a narrow way, i.e. due to loss aversion rather than other factors. The CVM method, specifically the dichotomous choice method, was used to elicit WTA and WTP.	The mean value of the WTA-WTP gap was 3.74, a result not of loss aversion, but of actions driven by the respondents' strategic motives.
Bao and Gong (2016)	Field experiment in China in 2013 (N=567). The endowment effect is defined as the WTA-WTP gap in a narrow way. The CVM method, specifically an open-ended question, was used to elicit WTA and WTP.	The average WTA was RMB 4,264,664 and the average WTP was RMB 4,140,140 which translates into a WTA-WTP gap of 1.03. The gap is higher during the upward momentum of the property market.
Gong et al. (2019)	Online experiment in China in 2016 (N=348). The endowment effect is defined as the WTA-WTP gap in a narrow way. The CVM method, specifically an open-ended question, was used to elicit WTA and WTP.	On average, the WTA is RMB 29,815 higher than the WTP.
Bao (2020)	Lab-in-the-field experiment in the UK (N=319). The endowment effect is defined as the WTA-WTP gap in a narrow way. The CVM method, specifically an open-ended question, was used to elicit WTA and WTP.	The endowment effect only occurs when prices in the housing market fall. In this case, WTA is on average 5% higher than WTP.

(Continued)

Table 1.2 (Continued)

Author	Methods	Results
Liu et al. (2021)	Field survey in China in 2018 (N=878). The endowment effect is defined as the WTA-WTP gap in a mixed way (strategic motivations were excluded, but the substitution effect was deliberately included). The CVM method, specifically an open-ended question, was used to elicit WTA and WTP.	The mean value of the WTA-WTP gap was 3.89. The strength of the endowment effect depends on the degree of emotional attachment to the property, the status of property rights and the villagers' livelihood substitutability.
Mwanyepedza and Mishi (2024)	Online survey in South Africa in 2022 (N=200). The endowment effect was defined as the WTA-WTP gap in a broad manner. The CVM method, specifically an open-ended question, was used to elicit WTA and WTP.	On average, the WTA is ZAR 234,200 higher than the WTP. The WTA-WTP gap disappears when hidden positive information about a property is revealed to buyers and negative information to sellers.

Source: Own study.

be willing to accept as compensation as a result of the expropriation of their property (WTA). In both cases, respondents declared values for their property where they live, so the experiment was not hypothetical, but rather based on real-life examples. He and Asami (2014) found that the average WTA-WTP gap was 3.74; however, according to the authors, this was an effect of respondents' strategic motives rather than an endowment effect based on loss aversion.

Nash and Rosenthal (2014) also investigated the endowment effect for housing goods in real-life settings. They used the natural division of students created through their participation in the College Housing Lottery. Some students were given the opportunity to live in their first-choice residences, whereas others were denied. Students who were given their first choice were asked about the minimum price they would accept to give up the opportunity of first-choice hall residence (WTA). Conversely, students who were not awarded were asked about the highest amount they would be willing to pay to obtain their first-choice residence (WTP). The results indicated that the mean WTA was 5.74, the mean WTP was 2.79, and the latter was statistically lower than the former. Nash and Rosenthal (2014) also demonstrated that the WTA-WTP gap widened over time as a result of the housing experience of students.

Bao and Gong (2016) focused on analysing the endowment effect during standard transactions in the sales housing market. The authors highlighted the fact that buyers and sellers set WTA and WTP values based on reference prices, i.e. the initial purchase price of the property and the market price of a similar property. Bao and Gong (2016) also stressed the problem of cycles in the housing market, in particular the timing of price increases and decreases. Ultimately, according to Bao and Gong (2016), the endowment effect can be expressed as

$$WTA - WTP = (w_s - w_b) \times (P_0 - P_{sm}) \tag{1}$$

where: w_s (w_b) is the weight assigned by the seller (buyer) to the initial purchase price of the property P_0, P_{sm} is the market price of a similar property. When the market is down, then $P_0 - P_{sm} > 0$ and $w_s - w_b > 0$, because sellers place a higher weighting to the initial price compared to buyers. For sellers, a transaction at the market price would imply a loss, so they are not willing to do so and therefore attach themselves to P_0. In turn, when the market is up, then $P_0 - P_{sm} < 0$ and $w_s - w_b < 0$, because buyers put a higher weighting to the initial price. In both cases $WTA - WTP > 0$, which indicates the presence of endowment effect. According to this theory, the values of WTA and WTP are between P_0 and P_{sm}. The empirical study by Bao and Gong (2016) is based on a field experiment that assumes hypothetical housing market transactions between standard buyers and sellers. The results indicate that the endowment effect shapes the behaviour of real estate market participants in Beijing, and is significantly higher during market price increases. The study showed that the endowment effect is moderated by the respondent's income level, employment situation, and attachment to ownership as a form of housing tenure.

In another study of the Beijing housing market, Gong et al. (2019) noted that the final reference point in the context of WTA and WTP value creation may be the expected price of the property. Gong et al. (2019) also suggested that the reference point may change as a result of the implementation of the policy instrument, for example, a law requiring the disclosure of all information like defects of a dwelling or the building in which it is located. The findings confirmed Bao and Gong's (2016) earlier analysis of the existence of the endowment effect in Beijing. However, in this case, the market cycle did not play a role in shaping the WTA-WTP gap, as opposed to the respondent's income level, age, gender, the quality of the property's neighbourhood, and its location.

Bao (2020) investigated the endowment effect in the United Kingdom (UK) housing market, using a lab-in-the-field experiment based on hypothetical scenarios. The study itself was very similar to that of Bao and Gong (2016); however, the results obtained were significantly different. First, in the UK housing market, the endowment effect occurs only during a downward price trend. Bao (2020) argues that sellers might overcome this behavioural bias during an upward cycle because their market is in the gain domain.

Liu et al. (2021) assessed the impact of the endowment effect on the withdrawal from rural homesteads (WRH) mechanism in China, which aims to relocate residents of rural homesteads to high-rise buildings. The researchers used a field survey to conduct the analysis by asking villagers about both WTA (minimum withdrawal price from homesteads) and WTP (maximum price that they would be willing to pay for their homestead if they rented it from someone else). The results showed that the mean WTA-WTP gap was 3.89 and that the endowment effect was moderated by emotional attachment to property, property rights status, and villagers' livelihood substitutability.

Mwanyepedza and Mishi (2024) identified the endowment effect in South Africa using an online survey. The results indicate that the WTA-WTP gap averages ZAR 234,200 and is statistically significant. However, it disappears when buyers receive previously hidden positive information about the property, whereas sellers receive negative information. The authors indicate that information asymmetry plays an important role in creating the endowment effect, treating this effect as the WTA-WTP gap in its broad sense. The results also revealed that the endowment effect is moderated by the income and gender of the respondents, as well as the physical characteristics of the dwelling and neighbourhood in which it is located.

1.2.4   Lessons learned and research gaps

This section intends to answer the research questions posed at the beginning of this chapter, based on the literature review.

RQ1. Has the endowment effect been identified in existing housing studies? If so, which factors moderate the strength of the endowment effect?

On the basis of all empirical studies to date analysing the endowment effect in the housing market, it can be concluded that this behavioural bias significantly affects its operation. In general, the endowment effect causes an overvaluation of housing goods (valuation paradigm), which reduces the number of transactions in the market and the housing mobility of the population (exchange paradigm). In addition to typical market activities, the endowment effect influences the effectiveness of public policies, especially those concerning the expropriation of real estate.

The endowment effect is not a constant quantity, and its strength is moderated by several factors. In the context of the housing market, the literature to date has highlighted, among other things, the issue of the current cycle of the market. However, the results are inconclusive across studies. Bao and Gong (2016) noticed a rise in the intensity of the WTA-WTP gap during price increases, while Bao (2020) observed it during price decreases. In turn, Gong et al. (2019) did not find a significant impact of the market cycle on the strength of the endowment effect. The latter effect is also influenced by respondents' characteristics, such as age, income level, employment situation or attachment to property ownership as a form of housing tenure. The research results also suggest that the endowment effect is a function of real estate rights specificity and available substitutes. It should be remembered that this last factor is treated as one of the fundamentals of the WTA-WTP gap in the framework of neoclassical economics and is not a moderator of the endowment effect in its narrow sense, that is, when it results from loss aversion.

RQ2. What are the challenges in measuring the endowment effect on housing goods?

Measuring the endowment effect in the housing market is associated with several constraints and challenges that can be categorised as (i) the choice of data collection method, (ii) defining the WTA-WTP gap, and (iii) multiple reference points.

Choice of data collection method

The WTA and WTP values necessary to identify the endowment effect within the valuation paradigm are not directly observable and must be elicited through experiments or surveys. Housing goods and the transactions of these goods are extremely complex, and for many households, the purchase of residential property is one of the most important decisions in their lives. Therefore, measuring the endowment effect through the most typical type of experiment, that is, a laboratory experiment, seems unrealistic (Bao, 2023). The laboratory experiment provides tight control of the environment, which maintains a high level of internal validity, but external validity is low, especially for complex markets such as housing markets. Therefore, to increase the external validity of the experiment, it is recommended to perform it in the field in the form of a typical field experiment or a lab-in-the-field experiment. The latter, compared to the former, is characterised by lower costs and less time to perform and is therefore increasingly used by behavioural researchers (Tomal & Brzezicka, 2022).

The WTA and WTP values have also been elicited through surveys in previous studies (Liu et al., 2021). However, in this case, survey participants were not randomly assigned to the control and treatment groups, which distorted the proportions of respondent characteristics in both groups and ultimately made it difficult to infer the effect of a given intervention on an outcome (Bao, 2023). In endowment effect research, surveys are often used in situations where respondents have to answer both WTA and WTP (He & Asami, 2014; Liu et al., 2021). In such a case, the WTA-WTP gap is highly likely to be underestimated, as respondents may not be able to immediately change their roles and adjust their responses accordingly.

The selection of suitable respondents has also received considerable attention in previous studies. In laboratory experiments, the subject pool usually consists of students who, however, according to Bao (2020), are not an appropriate group for assessing behavioural biases for complex products such as housing goods. On the other hand, a large proportion of students participate actively in housing market transactions, especially in the rental market (Mocanu & Tremacoldi-Rossi,

2023), but also in the sales market (De Gayardon et al., 2022). There-fore, the possibility of student participation during research on behav-ioural biases in the housing market should not be completely ruled out. There is also no consensus in the literature on whether respondents should be real homeowners. Bao and Gong (2016) argue that the re-search sample should not be narrowed in this regard, as doing so may reduce its representativeness. Conversely, Bao (2020) and Liu et al. (2021) emphasise the positive role of real decision makers' participa-tion in research.

Ultimately, when measuring the endowment effect in the housing market, researchers focus on whether the subject of the question is a fictitious or real residential property. The use of the former may make the scenarios presented less meaningful to the respondents (Nash & Rosenthal, 2014). On the other hand, the use of real properties, as done by Gong et al. (2019), requires very sophisticated experiments to be carried out to avoid situations where the respondents would have to act simultaneously as sellers and buyers. However, the endowment effect in the housing market was successfully identified in both cases.

Defining the WTA-WTP gap

In housing studies, much emphasis is placed on defining the WTA-WTP gap as a measure of the endowment effect. Both broad and narrow ap-proaches can be distinguished from each other. The former assumes that the endowment effect is directly the WTA-WTP gap regardless of its origin (e.g. the research by Nash and Rosenthal (2014)). How-ever, most studies have adopted a narrow approach to identify the endowment effect, in which only a part of the WTA-WTP gap based on loss aversion is attributed to this effect. The researchers adopted two methods to measure the narrow endowment effect. First, they at-tempted to design an experiment appropriately to eliminate other un-derpinnings of the WTA-WTP gap in advance. For example, He and Asami (2014) designed questions for respondents in such a way as to exclude the impact of transaction costs as well as income and substitu-tion effects on the WTA-WTP gap. In the survey, respondents were informed that transaction costs would be incurred independently. The questions on WTA and WTP explicitly stated that budget constraints (income effects) were disregarded. Moreover, the respondents were asked to estimate the amount for another house that was the same as the respondent's current house (substitution effect). He and Asami (2014), however, found that strategic motivations, rather than the endowment effect driven by loss aversion, were mainly responsible for the WTA-WTP gap. Liu et al. (2021) took this into account by instructing respondents that WTA and WTP values would only be used for research purposes. However, in this analysis, they did not attempt to remove the substitution effect upfront and instead treated it as a factor affecting the strength of the endowment effect.

Bao and Gong (2016) used a mixed method to remove cofounders of the WTA-WTP gap to identify the net endowment effect.[7] On the one hand, respondents were asked not to consider financial constraints when answering the questions. On the other hand, the researchers used a regression model in a difference-in-differences framework, which, by considering respondents' characteristics, indicated the impact of both the net endowment effect and other factors on the size of the WTA-WTP gap.

To examine the endowment effect using the WTA-WTP gap, Gong et al. (2019) considered that its size may depend on the magnitude of information asymmetry between buyers and sellers in the housing market, which is in line with Brown and Gregory's (1999) considerations. However, it should be emphasised that in standard experiments in which both parties to the transaction are asked about the same property, the problem of information asymmetry does not arise.

Multiple reference points

Sellers and buyers in housing markets have multiple reference points that influence their way of categorising a given transaction as either a loss or a gain and, consequently, the occurrence or not of the endowment effect. According to existing literature, these points can be grouped into the following areas: i) ownership/possession, ii) reference prices, iii) location and neighbourhood, and iv) social norms.

Within the first group, the primary reference point is the ownership or possession of the property, which causes sellers to treat the act of selling as a loss of part of their endowment and buyers as a gain as a result of adding a new good to their endowment (Morrison & Clark, 2016). The second category is based on reference prices as reference points. Bao and Gong (2016) confirmed that the reference points for the parties of the transaction are the initial purchase price of the property and the market price of a similar property. Further, Bao's (2020) results show that the WTA and WTP values also depend on the intermediate price (the price between the initial purchase price and the current market price) and, to a small extent, on the alternative price (the transaction price of a similar property). Gong et al. (2019) suggested that future property prices based on respondents' expectations of the development of the housing market may also be a reference point. Bao and Saunders (2023) concluded that, in the housing market, the reference prices for the parties to the transaction are the initial purchase price, intermediate price, alternative price, and expected price, which in this study was defined as the expected profit from the property transaction.[8] Another category relates to the location and neighbourhood of the property as reference points. Morrison and Clark (2016) were the first to highlight this. Specifically, people lump into their endowment not only the ownership/possession of a dwelling but also its location and neighbourhood, which Morrison and Clark (2016) called the locational status quo. The potential change of residence results in a subjective loss of this location and neighbourhood, which causes an aversion to residential mobility (in the exchange paradigm) and an increase in WTA (in the valuation paradigm). Finally, Bao and Saunders (2023) proposed that reference points for housing market transactions can be social norms manifested in the form of comparing oneself to given social groups (friends, colleagues, neighbours, and family).

RQ3. What are the research gaps in identifying the endowment effect in the housing market?

As indicated in the answer to question RQ2, the measurement of the endowment effect in the housing market is associated with several problems that arise from the complexity of housing and transactions involving these commodities. Therefore, research on the endowment effect in the housing market has been rather rare to date and still needs to be continued to better understand the nature of this behavioural bias in the market in question. The research gaps in the area under consideration can be grouped as follows: (i) measurement of the endowment effect, (ii) multiple reference points, and (iii) housing market segments.

Measurement of the endowment effect

Previous regression models that identify the net endowment effect in the housing market have fairly low explanatory power. For example, in the work of Bao and Gong (2016), the adjusted R^2 value was 0.107, whereas in the analysis by Gong et al. (2019), it was only 0.098. Thus, one can conclude that it is still necessary to look for both cofounders in the WTA-WTP gap and moderators of the net endowment effect in the housing market. In experiments where the object of study is not the same housing unit, it is worth considering the physical characteristics of the property that may significantly shape self-reported valuations (Tomal, 2022a). In this respect, some progress has been made in the work of Mwanyepedza and Mishi (2024). When property heterogeneity is eliminated during the experiment, more attention should be paid to better characterisation of the respondents. First, the WTA-WTP gap may not be due to the endowment effect understood in an economic sense (loss aversion) or in a psychological sense (attachment to the good) but is derived from the respondents' real housing situation. Martinelli and Parker (2009) specify that property overvaluation can result from a desire to avoid embarrassment or social stigma. If the latter two are firmly embedded in respondents' minds, they may also translate into their responses during hypothetical experiments. Tomal (2022b) also indicates that, in this context, higher self-reported valuations may be a consequence of the higher housing aspirations of this type of person. Future surveys should also take into account the neighbourhood and location of the respondents' place of residence. Again, these factors may be used, even subconsciously, by respondents to estimate WTA and WTP values. However, it should be noted that Gong et al. (2019) were the first to include basic location variables in the model specification.

Finally, research to date on the endowment effect has narrowed down to housing markets in a few countries, that is, Australia, South Africa, China, the US, and the UK, with research within the valuation paradigm conducted for the latter four. Maddux et al. (2010), however, indicated that the strength of the endowment effect differs between cultures. Furthermore, Wang et al. (2017) demonstrate that Hofstede's cultural dimensions significantly affect the level of loss aversion, which is the traditional driver of the endowment effect. Taking this into account, there is a lack of research in the existing literature for other countries, such as central and eastern European countries that have different cultural characteristics from Asian, African and Western countries.

Multiple reference points

Previous research on the endowment effect for housing goods has made a significant contribution to the understanding of the mechanism of the reference point. However, the nature of this phenomenon does not seem to have been explained comprehensively. First, the current literature does not indicate the validity of individual reference points in the housing market. Second, there are differences between the theoretical assumptions and empirical results. Bao and Gong's (2016) theory assumes that during a market decline, sellers should attach more importance to the initial purchase price and buyers to the market price. However, empirical results indicate that revealing the initial price of a property causes both buyers and sellers to change their WTA and WTP values in the same direction (Bao, 2020). Further research should clarify whether a poorly constructed data collection process, respondents' misunderstanding of the questions, or other psychological phenomena affecting the WTA-WTP value formation that researchers are not yet aware of may be responsible for this fact. Third, there is a lack of distinction in the housing literature to date as to which prices serve as reference points and which prices serve as the basis for self-valuations, along the lines of Weaver and Frederick's (2012) reference price theory. For example, for some sellers, the reference point may be the initial purchase price, and the market price may be the basis for their own valuation of the dwelling. The situation may be the opposite for others. Fourth, previous studies have considered the possibility of using price expectations as a reference point. In these studies, the expected price was a fixed future value of the property or a fixed expected profit from housing investment. Subsequent analyses may consider whether the expected price reference point in the housing market is stochastic according to the theory of Kőszegi and Rabin (2006). Ultimately, housing behavioural researchers should look for new reference points. For example, for housing developers, a reference point could be the sum of the construction costs and the purchase price of land (Nalepka & Tomal, 2016). Furthermore, in housing markets where substitution between homeownership and renting is low, a strong reference point could be the social norm, indicating that ownership is the "right" form of housing tenure (Lux & Sunega, 2022).

Housing market segments

Regarding the housing tenure criterion, the housing market can be divided into sales and rental markets. Further, within both these markets, a distinction can be made between primary and secondary markets, with newly built dwellings being traded in the former and previously used dwellings in the latter. This complexity of the housing market raises many directions for future analysis on the endowment effect. The manner in which the research to date has been conducted suggests that the endowment effect has only been analysed in terms of the sales secondary market while ignoring the sales primary market and the entire rental market.[9] However, the specifics of transactions across these markets are radically different in terms of the reference points and nature of the housing good. For example, in the primary market, the number of reference prices is less than that in the secondary market (there is no initial purchase price). Furthermore, in the primary market, for the seller/landlord, the dwelling will be more of an exchange rather than a consumption good, which raises the question of whether there is an endowment effect in this market. In addition, it appears that in the secondary rental market, the endowment effect will be weaker in the analogous sales market because the landlord can compensate for the loss of possession but retains a degree of control over the property through legal ownership. Moreover, in the secondary sales market, the endowment effect can be influenced by the purpose for which the dwelling was purchased. When sellers bought the property for investment purposes, their reference point was the expected profit from the investment. In summary, the complexity of the housing market means that the endowment effect can vary depending on the market segment and parties' objectives in relation to the transaction.

1.3   Summary

The endowment effect in the housing market has rarely been addressed by researchers. There have been only ten empirical papers in the literature to date, with three dealing with the endowment effect within the exchange paradigm and seven within the valuation paradigm. However, the results across publications have proven to be generally consistent, that is, the endowment effect is present in the housing market, but its strength can be moderated by various factors, including, but not limited to, the real estate market cycle and respondent characteristics.

Previous studies have also revealed that measuring the endowment effect in the housing market is associated with several difficulties. First, typical laboratory experiments are not suitable for collecting data for complex goods, such as housing. Further, the research process must be designed in such a way as to exclude other potential drivers of the

WTA-WTP gap. In the housing market, the latter involves income and substitution effects, transaction costs, strategic motives and information asymmetry. Furthermore, housing market transactions are so complex that potential sellers and buyers have multiple reference points. Consequently, hypothesising the occurrence of the endowment effect and its magnitude is made much more difficult because, under one reference point, a party to a transaction may experience the transaction as a loss and under the next reference point as a gain.

The literature review made it possible to identify several research gaps regarding the endowment effect in the housing market. First, additional cofounders of the WTA-WTP gap and moderators of the endowment effect should be sought because existing models have low explanatory power for this behavioural bias. Second, empirical studies have only focused on a few countries, mainly China, implying the need to identify the endowment effect in housing markets in other countries. Third, the theory of multiple reference points in housing markets must be unified. Fourth, the analyses so far have not taken into account the different segments of the housing market, so further research should attempt to identify the endowment effect, especially in the primary sales housing market, as well as in the primary and secondary rental markets, considering the unique characteristics of transactions in these markets.

Notes

1 According to standard economic theory, the rate of commodity substitution is the same in each direction, i.e. it does not matter whether there is a substitution of good A for B or B for A (Henderson & Quandt, 1971).

2 Hovenkamp (1991) proves that in the case of the WTA-WTP gap, assigning wealth to the person with the highest WTA maximises the wealth of society as follows: Suppose person *XYZ* has the maximum *WTA* value in society (WTA^{XYZ}) and person *ZYX* the highest *WTP* (WTP^{ZYX}), and the value of the remaining resources in society is V. When the good (G) is initially assigned to *ZYX*, then the social wealth is $V + WTP^{ZYX}$ because *XYZ* will not buy the good G from *ZYX* because $WTP^{XYZ} < WTP^{ZYX}$ and $WTA^{ZYX} \geq WTP^{ZYX}$, so $WTP^{XYZ} < WTA^{ZYX}$. On the other hand, when the good is initially assigned to person *XYZ* then the social wealth is $V + WTA^{XYZ}$ because $WTA^{XYZ} > WTP^{ZYX}$. In this case, good G should be assigned initially

to person *XYZ* because only in this way is social wealth maximised $(V + WTA^{XYZ} > V + WTP^{ZYX})$.

3 Given that housing studies on the endowment effect are dominated by the valuation paradigm, this chapter aims to explain the causes of the WTA-WTP gap in detail.

4 The construct of transaction demand can be categorised as a motivational factor rather than a psychological factor.

5 The Kőszegi and Rabin (2006) model also allows for multiple reference points to be considered when assessing the endowment effect.

6 Though real estate expropriation activities are not of a market nature and, strictly speaking, are not part of the housing market, it was decided not to omit this type of research. This is because the design of this type of research, as well as the idea of measuring the endowment effect, is not much different from research analysing the endowment effect during market transactions.

7 Bao and Gong (2016) called the loss aversion part of the WTA-WTP gap the net endowment effect. Chatterjee et al. (2013) adopted the idea that the ownership account is the cause of the endowment effect, independent of loss aversion.

8 Bao and Saunders (2023) did not study the endowment effect but only the effect of reference prices on the values of WTA and WTP.

9 Nash and Rosenthal (2014) in their study analysed the quasi-rental market present in student accommodation. Morrison and Clark (2016) predicted that, in theory, the endowment effect may also play a role in the rental market.

References

Alonso, W. (1960). A theory of the urban land market. *Papers and Proceedings of the Regional Science Association, 6*(1), 149–158. https://doi.org/10.1111/j.1435-5597.1960.tb01710.x

Ariely, D., Huber, J., & Wertenbroch, K. (2005). When do losses loom larger than gains? *Journal of Marketing Research, 42*(2), 134–138. https://doi.org/10.1509/jmkr.42.2.134.62283

Bao, H. X. (2020). *Behavioural science and housing decision making*. Routledge.

Bao, H. X. (2023). Between carrots and sticks, from intentions to actions: Behavioural interventions for housing decisions. *Housing, Theory and Society*. https://doi.org/10.1080/14036096.2023.2267060

Bao, H. X., & Gong, C. M. (2016). Endowment effect and housing decisions. *International Journal of Strategic Property Management, 20*(4), 341–353. https://doi.org/10.3846/1648715X.2016.1192069

Bao, H. X., & Saunders, R. (2023). Reference dependence in the UK housing market. *Housing Studies*, *38*(7), 1191–1219. https://doi.org/10.1080/02673037.2021.1935767

Becker, G. M., DeGroot, M. H., & Marschak, J. (1964). Measuring utility by a single-response sequential method. *Behavioral Science*, *9*(3), 226–232. https://doi.org/10.1002/bs.3830090304

Brenner, L., Rottenstreich, Y., Sood, S., & Bilgin, B. (2007). On the psychology of loss aversion: Possession, valence, and reversals of the endowment effect. *Journal of Consumer Research*, *34*(3), 369–376. https://doi.org/10.1086/518545

Brown, T. C. (2005). Loss aversion without the endowment effect, and other explanations for the WTA–WTP disparity. *Journal of Economic Behavior & Organization*, *57*(3), 367–379. https://doi.org/10.1016/j.jebo.2003.10.010

Brown, T. C., & Gregory, R. (1999). Why the WTA–WTP disparity matters. *Ecological Economics*, *28*(3), 323–335. https://doi.org/10.1016/S0921-8009(98)00050-0

Carmon, Z., & Ariely, D. (2000). Focusing on the forgone: How value can appear so different to buyers and sellers. *Journal of Consumer Research*, *27*(3), 360–370. https://doi.org/10.1086/317590

Chatterjee, P., Irmak, C., & Rose, R. L. (2013). The endowment effect as self-enhancement in response to threat. *Journal of Consumer Research*, *40*(3), 460–476. https://doi.org/10.1086/671344

Cheung, K. S., Wong, S. K., & Chung, Y. Y. (2023). Endowment effects of shared ownership: Evidence from Hong Kong. *Housing, Theory and Society*. https://doi.org/10.1080/14036096.2023.2265356

Clark, W. A., & Lisowski, W. (2017). Prospect theory and the decision to move or stay. *Proceedings of the National Academy of Sciences*, *114*(36), E7432–E7440. https://doi.org/10.1073/pnas.1708505114

De Gayardon, A., Callender, C., & DesJardins, S. L. (2022). Does student loan debt structure young people's housing tenure? Evidence from England. *Journal of Social Policy*, *51*(2), 221–241. https://doi.org/10.1017/S004727942000077X

Dequech, D. (2006). The new institutional economics and the theory of behaviour under uncertainty. *Journal of Economic Behavior & Organization*, *59*(1), 109–131.

Egger, M., & Smith, G. D. (2001). Principles of and procedures for systematic reviews. In M. Egger, G. Smith, & D. Altman (Eds.), *Systematic reviews in health care: Meta-analysis in context* (pp. 23–42). BMJ. https://doi.org/10.1002/9780470693926.ch2

Engelmann, D., & Hollard, G. (2010). Reconsidering the effect of market experience on the "endowment effect". *Econometrica*, *78*(6), 2005–2019. https://doi.org/10.3982/ECTA8424

Ericson, K. M., & Fuster, A. (2014). The endowment effect. *Annual Review of Economics*, *6*(1), 555–579. https://doi.org/10.1146/annurev-economics-080213-041320

Gong, C. M., Lizieri, C., & Bao, H. X. (2019). "Smarter information, smarter consumers"? Insights into the housing market. *Journal of Business Research*, *97*, 51–64. https://doi.org/10.1016/j.jbusres.2018.12.036

Hanemann, W. M. (1991). Willingness to pay and willingness to accept: How much can they differ? *The American Economic Review*, *81*(3), 635–647.

He, Z., & Asami, Y. (2014). How do landowners price their lands during land expropriation and the motives behind it: An explanation from a WTA-WTP experiment in central Beijing. *Urban Studies*, *51*(2), 412–427. https://doi.org/10.1177/0042098013492227

Henderson, J. M., & Quandt, R. E. (1971). *Microeconomic theory*. McGraw-Hill.

Horowitz, J. K., & McConnell, K. E. (2002). A review of WTA-WTP studies. *Journal of Environmental Economics and Management*, *44*(3), 426–447. https://doi.org/10.1006/jeem.2001.1215

Hovenkamp, H. (1991). Legal policy and the endowment effect. *The Journal of Legal Studies*, *20*(2), 225–247.

Huck, S., Kirchsteiger, G., & Oechssler, J. (2005). Learning to like what you have–explaining the endowment effect. *The Economic Journal*, *115*(505), 689–702. https://doi.org/10.1111/j.1468-0297.2005.01015.x

Jacques, S. (1992). The endowment effect and the Coase theorem. *American Journal of Agricultural Economics*, *74*(5), 1316–1323. https://doi.org/10.2307/1242804

Kahneman, D. (1992). Reference points, anchors, norms, and mixed feelings. *Organizational Behavior and Human Decision Processes*, *51*(2), 296–312. https://doi.org/10.1016/0749-5978(92)90015-Y

Kahneman, D., Knetsch, J. L., & Thaler, R. H. (1990). Experimental tests of the endowment effect and the Coase theorem. *Journal of Political Economy*, *98*(6), 1325–1348.

Kahneman, D., & Tversky, A. (1979). Prospect theory: An analysis of decision under risk. *Econometrica*, *47*(2), 263–292. https://doi.org/10.2307/1914185

Knetsch, J. L. (1989). The endowment effect and evidence of nonreversible indifference curves. *The American Economic Review*, *79*(5), 1277–1284.

Knetsch, J. L., & Wong, W. K. (2009). The endowment effect and the reference state: Evidence and manipulations. *Journal of Economic Behavior & Organization*, *71*(2), 407–413. https://doi.org/10.1016/j.jebo.2009.04.015

Knutson, B., Wimmer, G. E., Rick, S., Hollon, N. G., Prelec, D., & Loewenstein, G. (2008). Neural antecedents of the endowment effect. *Neuron*, *58*(5), 814–822. https://doi.org/10.1016/j.neuron.2008.05.018

Kőszegi, B., & Rabin, M. (2006). A model of reference-dependent preferences. *The Quarterly Journal of Economics, 121*(4), 1133–1165. https://doi.org/10.1093/qje/121.4.1133

Kurt, D., & Inman, J. J. (2013). Mispredicting others' valuations: Self-other difference in the context of endowment. *Journal of Consumer Research, 40*(1), 78–89. https://doi.org/10.1086/668888

List, J. A. (2003). Does market experience eliminate market anomalies? *The Quarterly Journal of Economics, 118*(1), 41–71. https://doi.org/10.1162/00335530360535144

List, J. A. (2004). Substitutability, experience, and the value disparity: Evidence from the marketplace. *Journal of Environmental Economics and Management, 47*(3), 486–509. https://doi.org/10.1016/j.jeem.2003.05.001

Liu, R., Jiang, J., Yu, C., Rodenbiker, J., & Jiang, Y. (2021). The endowment effect accompanying villagers' withdrawal from rural homesteads: Field evidence from Chengdu, China. *Land Use Policy, 101*, 105107. https://doi.org/10.1016/j.landusepol.2020.105107

Loewenstein, G., & Issacharoff, S. (1994). Source dependence in the valuation of objects. *Journal of Behavioral Decision Making, 7*(3), 157–168. https://doi.org/10.1002/bdm.3960070302

Lux, M., & Sunega, P. (2022). Pragmatic socioeconomics: A way towards new findings on sources of (housing) market instability. *Housing, Theory and Society, 39*(2), 129–146. https://doi.org/10.1080/14036096.2020.1853226

MacDonald, H. F., & Bowker, J. M. (1994). The endowment effect and WTA: A quasi-experimental test. *Journal of Agricultural and Applied Economics, 26*(2), 545–551. https://doi.org/10.1017/S1074070800026456

Maddux, W. W., Yang, H., Falk, C., Adam, H., Adair, W., Endo, Y., . . . & Heine, S. J. (2010). For whom is parting with possessions more painful? Cultural differences in the endowment effect. *Psychological Science, 21*(12), 1910–1917. https://doi.org/10.1177/0956797610388818

Mandel, D. R. (2002). Beyond mere ownership: Transaction demand as a moderator of the endowment effect. *Organizational Behavior and Human Decision Processes, 88*(2), 737–747. https://doi.org/10.1016/S0749-5978(02)00013-4

Martinelli, C., & Parker, S. W. (2009). Deception and misreporting in a social program. *Journal of the European Economic Association, 7*(4), 886–908. https://doi.org/10.1162/JEEA.2009.7.4.886

Menard, C., & Shirley, M. M. (2005). Introduction. In C. Menard & M. M. Shirley (Eds.), *Handbook of new institutional economics* (pp. 1–18). Springer.

Mocanu, T., & Tremacoldi-Rossi, P. (2023). The impact of international students on housing markets. *Canadian Journal of Economics/Revue canadienne d'économique*, *56*(2), 647–675. https://doi.org/10.1111/caje.12651

Morewedge, C. K., & Giblin, C. E. (2015). Explanations of the endowment effect: An integrative review. *Trends in Cognitive Sciences*, *19*(6), 339–348. https://doi.org/10.1016/j.tics.2015.04.004

Morrison, P. S., & Clark, W. A. (2016). Loss aversion and duration of residence. *Demographic Research*, *35*, 1079–1100. https://doi.org/10.4054/DemRes.2016.35.36

Mwanyepedza, R., & Mishi, S. (2024). Endowment effect, information asymmetry, and real estate market decisions: Willingness to pay and willingness to accept disparities. *Real Estate Management and Valuation*, *32*(1), 37–48. https://doi.org/10.2478/remav-2024-0004

Nalepka, A., & Tomal, M. (2016). Identyfikacja czynników kształtujących ceny ofertowe deweloperskich lokali mieszkalnych na obszarze jednostki ewidencyjnej Nowa Huta. *Świat Nieruchomości*, *96*, 11–18. https://doi.org/10.14659/worej.2016.96.02

Nash, J. G., & Rosenthal, R. A. (2014). An investigation of the endowment effect in the context of a college housing lottery. *Journal of Economic Psychology*, *42*, 74–82. https://doi.org/10.1016/j.joep.2014.01.001

Nightingale, A. (2009). A guide to systematic literature reviews. *Surgery (Oxford)*, *27*(9), 381–384. https://doi.org/10.1016/j.mpsur.2009.07.005

Novemsky, N., & Kahneman, D. (2005). The boundaries of loss aversion. *Journal of Marketing Research*, *42*(2), 119–128. https://doi.org/10.1509/jmkr.42.2.119.62292

Page, M. J., McKenzie, J. E., Bossuyt, P. M., Boutron, I., Hoffmann, T. C., Mulrow, C. D., . . . & Moher, D. (2021). The PRISMA 2020 statement: An updated guideline for reporting systematic reviews. *International Journal of Surgery*, *88*, 105906. https://doi.org/10.1136/bmj.n71

Pierce, J. L., Kostova, T., & Dirks, K. T. (2003). The state of psychological ownership: Integrating and extending a century of research. *Review of General Psychology*, *7*(1), 84–107. https://doi.org/10.1037/1089-2680.7.1.84

Reb, J., & Connolly, T. (2007). Possession, feelings of ownership and the endowment effect. *Judgment and Decision Making*, *2*(2), 107–114. https://doi.org/10.1017/S1930297500000085

Rosato, A. (2016). Selling substitute goods to loss-averse consumers: Limited availability, bargains, and rip-offs. *The RAND Journal of Economics*, *47*(3), 709–733. https://doi.org/10.1111/1756-2171.12139

Shogren, J. F., Cho, S., Koo, C., List, J., Park, C., Polo, P., & Wilhelmi, R. (2001). Auction mechanisms and the measurement of WTP and

WTA. *Resource and Energy Economics, 23*(2), 97–109. https://doi.org/10.1016/S0928-7655(00)00038-5

Shu, S. B., & Peck, J. (2011). Psychological ownership and affective reaction: Emotional attachment process variables and the endowment effect. *Journal of Consumer Psychology, 21*(4), 439–452. https://doi.org/10.1016/j.jcps.2011.01.002

Sprenger, C. (2015). An endowment effect for risk: Experimental tests of stochastic reference points. *Journal of Political Economy, 123*(6), 1456–1499. https://doi.org/10.1086/683836

Strahilevitz, M. A., & Loewenstein, G. (1998). The effect of ownership history on the valuation of objects. *Journal of Consumer Research, 25*(3), 276–289. https://doi.org/10.1086/209539

Thaler, R. (1980). Toward a positive theory of consumer choice. *Journal of Economic Behavior & Organization, 1*(1), 39–60. https://doi.org/10.1016/0167-2681(80)90051-7

Tomal, M. (2022a). Drivers behind the accuracy of self-reported home valuations: Evidence from an emerging economy. *Journal of European Real Estate Research, 15*(3), 425–443. https://doi.org/10.1108/JERER-02-2022-0004

Tomal, M. (2022b). The applicability of self-reported home values in housing wealth inequality assessment: Evidence from an emerging country. *Housing Studies.* https://doi.org/10.1080/02673037.2022.2123902

Tomal, M., & Brzezicka, J. (2022). Certainty equivalent, risk attitudes and housing. *Applied Economics Letters, 30*(18), 2576–2580. https://doi.org/10.1080/13504851.2022.2099797

Tversky, A., & Kahneman, D. (1991). Loss aversion in riskless choice: A reference-dependent model. *The Quarterly Journal of Economics, 106*(4), 1039–1061. https://doi.org/10.2307/2937956

Tversky, A., & Kahneman, D. (1992). Advances in prospect theory: Cumulative representation of uncertainty. *Journal of Risk and Uncertainty, 5*, 297–323. https://doi.org/10.1007/BF00122574

Van Dijk, E., & Van Knippenberg, D. (1996). Buying and selling exchange goods: Loss aversion and the endowment effect. *Journal of Economic Psychology, 17*(4), 517–524. https://doi.org/10.1016/0167-4870(96)00017-7

Vickrey, W. (1961). Counterspeculation, auctions, and competitive sealed tenders. *The Journal of Finance, 16*(1), 8–37. https://doi.org/10.2307/2977633

Wang, M., Rieger, M. O., & Hens, T. (2017). The impact of culture on loss aversion. *Journal of Behavioral Decision Making, 30*(2), 270–281. https://doi.org/10.1002/bdm.1941

Weaver, R., & Frederick, S. (2012). A reference price theory of the endowment effect. *Journal of Marketing Research*, *49*(5), 696–707. https://doi.org/10.1509/jmr.09.0103

Willig, R. D. (1976). Consumer's surplus without apology. *The American Economic Review*, *66*(4), 589–597.

Yan, J., & Bao, H. X. (2018). A prospect theory-based analysis of housing satisfaction with relocations: Field evidence from China. *Cities*, *83*, 193–202. https://doi.org/10.1016/j.cities.2018.06.022

2 Endowment effects in housing markets

Theoretical grounds

Chapter overview

This chapter partly responds to the identified research gaps presented
in Chapter 1 in studies on the endowment effect and housing market. In particular, it aims to develop a theoretical model explaining
the magnitude of endowment effects in the sales and rental housing
markets, with a distinction between primary and secondary markets.
Inductive reasoning is used to achieve the aim of the chapter, in particular, by starting with an assessment of the impact of the various reference points on the development of bids and offer prices of residential
properties and ending with the development of a theoretical model.
The discussion of the size of the endowment effect is preceded by a
description of the basics of the housing market to understand its functioning from the perspective of mainstream economics. The theoretical model presented suggests that sellers/landlords and buyers/tenants,
when estimating the price/rent of a residential property, consider the
nature of the transacted good (exchangeable/consumable) and have
multiple reference points. It is postulated that the endowment effect
will be lowered in primary markets (sales and rental) where sellers/
landlords treat housing as goods for sale/rent, and therefore, they do
not demand additional compensation for the loss of property ownership and/or possession. However, in this case, sellers/landlords can
adjust their property self-valuations depending on the reference prices.
The strongest endowment effect is likely to occur in the secondary
sales market, where sellers use dwellings for consumption purposes. In
turn, in the secondary rental market, the endowment effect is predicted
to occur but will be weaker than in the sales market, as the landlord
making the transaction only compensates for the loss of possession

DOI: 10.1201/9781003512004-3

over the property, rather than possession and legal ownership. In summary, this chapter answers the following research questions.

RQ4. From a theoretical perspective, what are the reference points in housing transactions and how do they affect the formation of the endowment effect in the housing market?

RQ5. According to the theory, does the strength of endowment effects differ between sales and rental housing markets and across primary and secondary markets?

2.1 The essence of the housing market

2.1.1 *Housing goods and the housing market*

Housing goods have several unique characteristics. Fallis (1985) distinguished the following features of housing goods: heterogeneity, durability, and spatial fixity.[1] The first feature, i.e. heterogeneity, means that properties vary widely in their physical characteristics (e.g. floor area, number of rooms), neighbourhood (e.g. distance to school) and location (e.g. distance to city centre). This heterogeneity makes it difficult to define and measure the unit of supply and demand in the market as well as to determine the price during a transaction. However, some housing economists do not consider the heterogeneity of housing goods. For example, Olsen (1969) introduced an unobservable construct called housing service by assuming that the price per unit of housing service is the same for all housing units. Consequently, the differences between housing prices are only due to the number of units of housing services they provide to households (Fallis, 1985).

The second feature of housing goods is durability, meaning that housing stock can provide housing services to households for many years. The term housing stock, which refers to the number of dwellings in an area, should be separated from the housing service construct. On this basis, two housing markets can be distinguished: the housing service market, where the price per unit of housing services is determined, and the housing stock market, where the price per unit of housing stock is determined. These two markets, treating housing as a consumption good and an investment good, respectively, are closely related in the sense that the value of the housing stock is estimated based on the flows of housing services it can provide. Specifically, the value of housing stock is equal to the sum of the discounted flows of the housing services that it delivers. Housing services can generally be served to a household through the purchase of housing stock or its rental, which makes it possible to distinguish the ownership market, also known as the sales market, from the rental market as separate segments of the housing market using housing tenure as a criterion. In housing economics, the cost of acquiring housing services through ownership is defined as the user cost which is the product of the price of housing stock and the interest rate. In equilibrium with perfect markets, the user cost is equal to the rent; thus, households become indifferent towards acquiring housing services through ownership or renting. However, empirical observations show that housing markets are not perfect, and the cost of acquiring housing services differs across sales and rental markets (Fallis, 1985).

The third feature of housing goods is spatial fixity, meaning that, in general, housing cannot be moved from one place to another. Therefore, the purchaser of a housing unit is not just buying strictly the housing unit, but also in a sense its neighbourhood and location. Therefore, prices per unit of housing service will vary over space, and consumers will be willing to pay a higher price for dwellings closer to the city centre. However, neighbourhood and location may generate positive or negative externalities that further influence the price of a housing unit.

The housing market brings together the demand and supply for housing, resulting in sales and rental transactions (Oxley & Haffner, 2012). Green and Malpezzi (2003) argued that the housing market consists of inputs, supply-side agents, and demand-side agents. Inputs such as land, labour, capital, materials, and infrastructure, together with supply-side agents, produce housing services. Supply-side agents include developers, builders, landlords, homeowners and renters. Developers and builders provide housing services to the market by creating a new housing stock for sale. Landlords, on the other hand, operate on the existing housing stock and allocate it for rent. Homeowners and renters can also, to a small extent, be considered supply-side agents who produce housing services as they maintain and upgrade their homes. Finally, on the demand-side agents, homeowners and tenants purchase housing services at appropriate prices (rents). In this context, the housing good is consumption in nature; that is, the focus is on housing services. However, as previously mentioned, housing can also be treated as an investment good, making the housing stock the object of the transaction, with the price of the latter determined by the value of housing services. Based on these premises, four main segments of the housing market can be distinguished according to the criteria of housing tenure and newness of the housing stock:

- Primary sales housing market – this is the market where ownership rights to newly built residential properties are transferred,
- Secondary sales housing market – this is the market where ownership rights to previously used residential properties are transferred,
- Primary rental housing market – this is the market where rental contracts are concluded to newly built residential properties,
- Secondary rental housing market – this is the market where rental contracts are concluded to previously used residential properties.

Fallis (1985) highlights two additional features of the housing market. First, the housing market has high transaction costs and information asymmetry. The former means that relocation is costly in terms of time, money, and emotions, making housing markets slow to adjust to changes in household income. Information asymmetry means that the parties to a transaction have different information resources. Households do not have complete information on the characteristics of the dwellings being sold, while sellers usually do not have information on the bid prices of potential buyers.

2.1.2   *Demand and supply for housing*

Treating a dwelling as a heterogeneous good, one can represent it as a vector of $(z_1,..,z_n)$ observable and measurable characteristics, which include its physical features, neighbourhood and location. This concept was developed by Rosen (1974), whose approach indicates that the housing services of a dwelling can be broken down into numerous attributes associated with the property (Adair et al., 1996). In the market, there is a price $p(\mathbf{z}) = p(z_1,..,z_n)$, which is closely related to the vector of given characteristics. In the rental market, the price $p(\mathbf{z})$ is a transactional rent while in the sales market a transaction price. These assumptions allow us to conclude that households can buy different bundles of housing attributes in the housing market at their associated prices. Fallis (1985) concretises that $p(\mathbf{z})$ is the minimum price at which a given housing attribute bundle can be bought. A households choose such a bundle of attributes $(z_1,..,z_n)$ that maximises its utility function $u = u(v_1, z_1,.., z_n)$ where v_1 is a composite good. The u function has a budget constraint $y = p_1 v_1 + p(\mathbf{z})$ where p_1 is the price of a composite good v_1. A bid function $\theta(z_1,..,z_n|u,y)$ shows how much a household is willing to pay for a set of characteristics $(z_1,..,z_n)$ at a given level of utility u and income y. For different levels of values of characteristic z_1 and fixed values of $(z_2,..,z_n)$ part of the bid function is of the form $\theta(z_1,z_2',..,z_n'|u,y)$. Similarly, the part of the $p(\mathbf{z})$ function has the form $p(\mathbf{z}) = p(z_1,z_2',..,z_n')$ and it represents the prices for different quantities of the characteristic z_1, with other attributes fixed. The slope of the part of bid function for z_1 is the marginal rate of substitution between z_1 and other things. The slope of $p(z_1,z_2',..,z_n')$ denotes the marginal rate at which the family can substitute the characteristic z_1 and other things in the market. In this case, the maximisation of a household utility will occur when the parts of the bid function and the market function for z_1 are tangent to each other (see Figure 2.1).

On the supply side, there is the problem of profit maximisation considering the market function $p(\mathbf{z})$ and the production cost $c(z_1,..,z_n,q)$

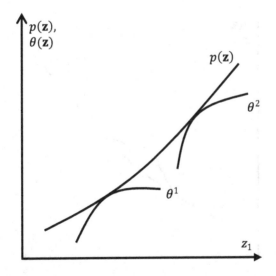

Figure 2.1 Maximum household utility for characteristic z_1.

Source: Adapted from Fallis (1985).

Note: There are different bid functions between households. The figure illustratively shows two bid functions.

where q is the number of housing units with characteristics $(z_1,..,z_n)$. Consequently, a housing stock production company has an offer function $\vartheta(z_1,..,z_n \mid pr)$, where pr is the company profit. The offer function reports the price the company is willing to accept for a housing unit with given characteristics (Fallis, 1985). Finally, profit maximisation for characteristic z_1 at fixed values of the other attributes occurs when the offer function is tangent to the market function $p(\mathbf{z})$ (see Figure 2.2).

2.1.3   Market equilibrium for heterogeneous housing goods

Under the assumption that housing goods are heterogeneous, equilibrium in the housing market occurs when all offer functions of housing services producers and all bid functions of households are tangent to the market function $p(\mathbf{z})$ as in Figure 2.3. Households have different bid functions because they differ in their preferences and incomes. Similarly, producers differ in their input prices, efficiency, and production functions, resulting in various offer functions (Fallis, 1985).

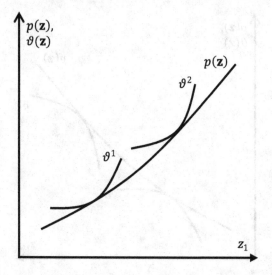

Figure 2.2 Maximum company profit for characteristic z_1.

Source: Adapted from Fallis (1985).

Note: There are different offer functions between producers. The figure illustratively shows two offer functions.

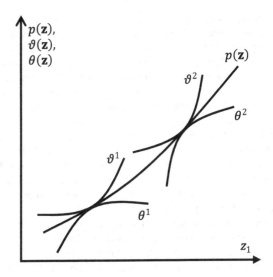

Figure 2.3 Housing market equilibrium for characteristic z_1.

Source: Adapted from Fallis (1985).

Given all this, finding market equilibrium means identifying the function $p(\mathbf{z})$ for which housing supply equals housing demand for characteristics $(z_1, .., z_n)$. The partial derivative of the function $p(\mathbf{z})$ for characteristic z_i is defined as the hedonic price at which the market cleaning process occurs (Goodman, 1983). Empirical estimation of the function $p(\mathbf{z})$ is made by regressing real estate transaction prices (for the sales market) or contracted rents (for the rental market) on the physical, neighbourhood and location characteristics of the properties. Malpezzi (2003) for a hedonic function on the housing market suggests using a log-linear form since it allows for differentiation in the value of individual characteristics, simple interpretation of the coefficients obtained, and elimination of the problem of variable variance of the error term. In addition, log-linear models are not computationally demanding and are characterised by specification flexibility.

These considerations indicate that in equilibrium in the housing market, the WTP values of buyers and WTA values of sellers are equal to each other, and both are equal to the market price P_m determined by the function $p(\mathbf{z})$ (Cotteleer et al., 2008; Bao & Gong,

2016). Standard housing economic theory assumes that people are reference-independent when making decisions; that is, they have no reference points. The literature review in Chapter 1 indicates that the this assumption does not hold, resulting in the WTA-WTP gap, which is a manifestation of the endowment effect. From the point of view of behavioural economics, the market function $p(\mathbf{z})$ includes not only objective variables describing the characteristics of a property, such as its physical features or neighbourhood attributes, but also subjective ones (Smith, 2011). Among others, Levy et al. (2008) stress that the emotions associated with property should also be added to the vector of attributes $\mathbf{z}$. Another approach was proposed by Boelhouwer (2011), who suggested the inclusion of a temporally lagged dependent variable to capture the speculative behaviour of residential consumers.

The WTA-WTP gap causes friction in the market, which disrupts the cleaning process. In this case, the bid functions of households and the offer functions of housing producers are not tangent to each other; rather, there is a gap between them, as shown in Figure 2.4. For example, in Figure 2.4a, WTA is higher than WTP, and the latter is equal to or close to the market price P_m. Other possible situations for the occurrence of the WTA-WTP gap in the housing market are shown in Figure 2.4b-e.

2.2 A conceptual model of endowment effects across sales and rental housing markets

Chapter 1 indicates that housing transaction parties have multiple reference points, which can be grouped into the following categories: 1) reference prices, 2) ownership/possession, 3) location and neighbourhood, and 4) social norms. To develop a theoretical model to explain the endowment effects across sales and rental housing markets, taking into account the division between primary and secondary markets, this perspective of multiple reference points is applied.

2.2.1 The role of reference points

Reference prices as reference points

Previous research indicates that during housing transactions, the reference prices for parties can be the initial purchase price, intermediate price, alternative transaction/bid price, and expected price (Bao &

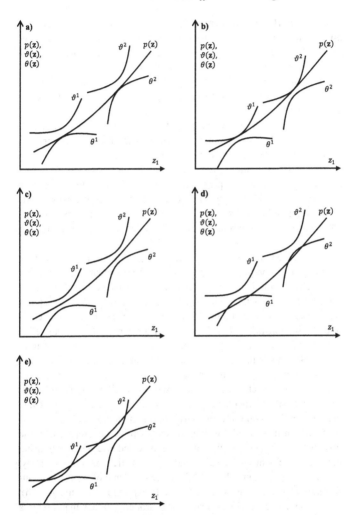

Figure 2.4 Housing market imbalance for characteristic z_1 as a result of the endowment effect.

Source: Own study.

Note: a) $WTA > WTP$ with $WTP = P_m$ and $WTA > P_m$; b) $WTA > WTP$ with $WTP < P_m$ and $WTA = P_m$; c) $WTA > WTP$ with $WTP < P_m$ and $WTA > P_m$; d) $WTA > WTP$ with $WTP > P_m$ and $WTA > P_m$; e) $WTA > WTP$ with $WTP < P_m$ and $WTA < P_m$.

Gong, 2016; Bao & Saunders, 2023). However, previous studies have not considered the fact that transactions in the housing market may have different characteristics depending on whether the sales or rental market is analysed, as well as whether the primary or secondary market is the focus. In addition, the buying side of the transaction has less information about the property and, thus, will have fewer price reference points.

According to the reference price theory of Weaver and Frederick (2012), to explain the endowment effect, it is crucial to understand what price reference points the parties to the transaction adopt and what their self-valuations are for the good being transacted. Based on the hedonic price theory presented in the previous section, it can be assumed that for both buyers and sellers, the basis for their own valuation of a dwelling is its market price (P_m), which is generally calculated using transaction prices of similar properties in the local housing market.[2]

By contrast, the problem of transaction parties' price reference points is more complicated. For sellers in the secondary sales housing market, the natural first price reference point is the initial purchase price (P_o). As further price information is analysed, the reference point will successively become the intermediate price (P_n) and the alternative transaction price (P_a). However, it appears that the final reference point will be the expected price (P_e) as shown also in Gong et al. (2019). This is because research to date indicates that a significant proportion of the population makes decisions in the real estate market based on expectations of future market development (Głuszak & Rymarzak, 2019; Kuchler et al., 2023). It can be assumed that this postulate will become increasingly important as more information is presented in mass media in the context of price development in the housing market. The formulation of the expected price (P_e) by housing market participants is based on rather simplistic reasoning. Namely, buyers or sellers, on the basis of the price trend and other available information (such as interest rate policy and expected economic growth), determine a fixed expected price for a property, rather than create a stochastic reference point (the entire distribution of expected prices).[3]

In turn, in the primary sales market for sellers (de facto housing developers), the first reference point is the sum of the construction cost and land price, and the subsequent points are the same as for the seller in the secondary market. Again, the final reference point is the expected price (P_e), which is also indicated by empirical studies showing that housing developers take into account price expectations in order to shape their pricing policy (Wen et al., 2018). In the context of the rental market, it can also be assumed that potential landlords in both the primary and secondary markets will ultimately compare their self-valuations to price expectations, but in this respect, the focus is on the expected rent (R_e). Analogously to sellers, also for buyers in the housing market the final price reference point is the expected price (P_e). However, it should be emphasised that for the demand side of the market, the first point of reference is usually the alternative bid price (P_a), as buyers generally do not know information about the initial purchase price of the property or its intermediate price (P_n). The same applies to tenants for whom the final price reference point is the expected rent (R_e).

Taking these considerations into account, it is possible to determine how buyers/tenants and sellers/landlords will feel about a potential transaction given their self-valuations (V), i.e. P_m or R_m for the sales market and rental market, respectively, compared to the final price reference point (Z) which is the expected price (P_e) or expected rent (R_e). Weaver and Frederick (2012) point out that when $Z_s > V_s$ (up market) then a seller/landlord will not be willing to give up the good (in this case the dwelling) for V_s, but rather will demand more than V_s. In this case, selling/renting the dwelling at a price lower than the expected price/rent will be considered a loss (see Figure 2.5a), so the seller/landlord will demand some compensation for this loss. The size of this compensation should be large enough for sellers/landlords to bring the WTA level close to the reference price (see Figure 2.1 in Weaver and Frederick (2012)). On the other hand, during a down market, i.e. when $Z_s < V_s$ sellers/landlords are inclined to stay with their self-valuations and will view the transaction as a gain. For buyers/tenants when $Z_b < V_b$ (down market) then they are not willing to pay an amount equal to V_b for the dwelling, but rather a lower amount closer to the reference price. In the opposite situation when $Z_b > V_b$ (up market) buyers attach to V_b because they view the transaction as a gain (see Figure 2.5b).

Weaver and Frederick (2012) indicate that the magnitude of the price adjustment to V for both buyers and sellers is symmetric. To explain, suppose the buyer and seller have the same value of V, i.e. $V_s = V_b$. When the seller's reference point is larger by a unit than his/her V, the upward adjustment will be x. On the other hand, when the buyer's reference point is smaller than his/her V by a unit then the downward adjustment will be $-x$. Therefore, it is crucial to determine

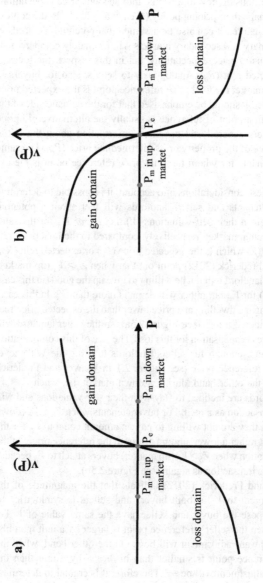

Figure 2.5 a) Prospect theory value function for sellers; b) Prospect theory value function for buyers.

Source: Adapted from Bao and Gong (2016) and Weaver and Frederick (2012).

whether buyers and sellers during down and up markets, respectively, tend to make similar predictions about the difference between V and the final price reference point (Z), which is the expected price (P_e) or expected rent (R_e). If sellers/landlords tend to make more extreme predictions on expected price/rent during the up market then their adjustments to V will be much higher than the analogous adjustments of buyers/tenants during the down market, because $(V_b - Z_b) < (Z_s - V_s)$. Weaver and Frederick (2012) suggested that transaction disutility tends to raise the selling price significantly more than it lowers the buying price, supporting this conjecture. In the context of the housing market, this position can be argued by the fact that during an up market, price increases are generally higher than analogous decreases during a down market due to phenomena such as fashion, hype, and trend chasing (Clayton, 1998).

It is difficult to determine whether price adjustments are greater for investors or consumers of housing goods. On the one hand, the former want to maximise their return on investment, which may result in an increased price correction to V. However, investors' aggressive negotiating tactics may be undermined in times of high inflation in the economy because of a quick desire to move cash into the property market. On the other hand, for consumers, the purchase of a home is one of the most important decisions in their lives and involves a large expense. Potential buyers will likely want to negotiate the lowest possible price for a dwelling to cover the future expenses associated with furnishing it.

Ownership/possession as a reference point

Behavioural researchers, when analysing the endowment effect, take legal ownership of the good and/or possession of the good, that is, the ability to exercise control over it, as the standard reference point. The loss of ownership/possession results in an increase in the price at which the seller is willing to give up the good because he/she must compensate for this loss (of legal ownership and/or possession). The empirical studies presented in Chapter 1 confirm that the ownership/possession reference point is important in housing market transactions. However, it should be emphasised that this does not occur during every transaction. First, in primary sales and rental markets, the housing good is exchangeable rather than consumable, so the seller's/landlord's reference point becomes "not having" because the good is no longer part of their endowment (Shu & Peck, 2011) (see Figure 2.6b). The price reference point is the dominant reference point for this type of seller/landlord. A similar situation will occur for a seller/landlord in the secondary market who has not consumed the housing good, and whose goal is to sell/rent it in order to achieve a return on investment. In these cases, compensation for giving away ownership or possession of the property is unlikely to occur, unlike for sellers/landlords of housing who resided in it.

The compensation for surrendering ownership and possession of property will differ between rental and sales markets. Specifically, in a transaction in the sales market, both legal ownership and possession of goods are eliminated. By contrast, in the rental market, only possession is given away, and the landlord is left with legal ownership. As can be seen in Figure 2.6a, the seller's disutility associated with a transaction in the sales market is greater (the difference between the ownership/possession reference point and the event resulting in no ownership and no possession) than the landlord's disutility in the rental market (the difference between the ownership/possession reference point and the event resulting in being only the owner). It should be noted that some publications, such as the work of Reb and Connolly (2007), postulate that the endowment effect is created only through the possession of goods. However, these studies have dealt with simple everyday items. With housing, this situation becomes much more complicated. Even in the absence of possession, the owner has a great deal of influence over property and is unlikely to remove it from his/her endowment altogether – this situation concerns a landlord who treated the dwelling as a consumer good.

Location and neighbourhood as reference points

Morrison and Clark (2016) postulate that people also have a locational reference point, which stems from their attachment to the neighbourhood and location of their dwellings. Yan and Bao (2018) pointed out this fact by defining the endowment effect as an attachment to the place of former residence. The psychological and housing literature supports this conclusion. For example, Hidalgo and Hernandez (2001) proved that people become attached to both the neighbourhood of their home and the city in which they live. This attachment can be both social and physical. The former refers to the de facto attachment to the people who live in the analysed space. Lewicka (2010) repeated and extended

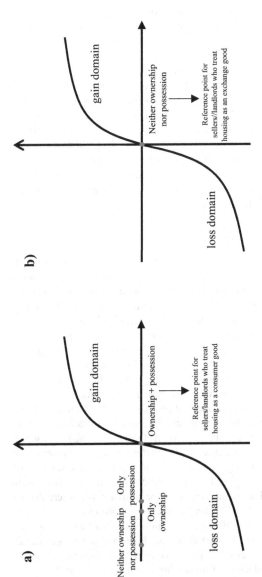

Figure 2.6 The ownership/possession reference point for sellers/landlords treating housing as a) a consumer good; b) an exchange good.

Source: Own study.

Note: Legal ownership and possession are marked close together, as it is not possible to state clearly whether it would be more painful for participants in the housing market to lose ownership or possession alone.

this analysis for Warsaw, Wroclaw, Lodz, and Lviv, examining attachment to homes, buildings, neighbourhoods, city districts, and cities. The results indicated that the lowest attachment was to the city district and the highest attachment to the home.

This research also paints a picture that attachment to the neighbourhood and location is an attribute only to the actual residents of dwellings. Consequently, when the owner of the property treats it as an exchange (non-resident) rather than a consumer good, this type of attachment will not occur, and, as a result, the seller/landlord will not experience a loss from the sale/rent of the dwelling and its associated neighbourhood and location. In summary, it can be assumed that only sellers/landlords who consume their dwellings include the neighbourhood and location in their endowments and will demand additional compensation for their loss.

Social norms as reference points

Bao and Saunders (2023) were the first to propose social norms as reference points for the housing market. These researchers argue that the nature of the housing market reinforces the likelihood that individuals socially compare themselves. Bao and Saunders (2023) focused specifically on comparing lifestyles between individuals but obtained weak evidence to support their hypothesis. An alternative reference point based on social norms for transacting parties may offer pragmatic socioeconomics developed by Lux et al. (2017) and Lux and Sunega (2022). This approach combines sociology and mainstream economics and seeks to explain the behaviour of real estate market participants. Specifically, pragmatic socioeconomics assumes that economically rational behaviour in the housing market is often constrained by an informal social norm regarding the "right" form of housing tenure which is ownership. In such a case, market participants prefer ownership to tenancy whenever they can afford it, regardless of all other factors. Lux et al. (2020) empirically confirmed that this informal social norm exists in many European countries, especially in those where the development of the rental housing market is at a low level.

The social norm of the right form of housing tenure can be a point of reference only in specific transactions in the housing market, that is, when a seller of a dwelling owns and uses it and then has to change the form of satisfaction of his/her housing needs and becomes a tenant. In this case, his/her reference point will be the socially right form of housing tenure which is ownership, and he/she will treat becoming a tenant as a loss for which he/she must compensate. Ultimately, this mechanism may cause an increase in the WTA. For housing exchange goods, the analysed social norm should not play any role since sellers satisfy their housing needs regardless of the object of the transaction.

2.2.2 Endowment effects across housing markets in theory

Given the reference points of the parties to the housing market transactions defined in the previous section and the characteristics presented at the beginning of this chapter, it is possible to determine the WTA-WTP gaps in the sales and rental housing markets by primary and secondary markets, making the following assumptions:

1. The WTA value can be expressed using the following general formula:

$$WTA = V + A_p + A_o + A_l + A_n \tag{2}$$

where V is a seller's/landlord's self-valuation taken as the property's market price (P_m) for the sales market or market rent (R_m) for the rental market, A_p is an adjustment due to the price reference point being the expected price (P_e) or expected rent (R_e), A_o is an adjustment due to the ownership/possession reference point, A_l is an adjustment due to the locational reference point, A_n is an adjustment due to the social norm reference point. For a seller, if $P_e > P_m$ (up market) then $(P_e - P_m) > A_p > 0$ and 0 otherwise (down market). An analogous situation exists in the rental market. In addition, A_o and A_l is greater than 0 only for sellers/landlords who consume their dwellings, and is equal to 0 otherwise. Finally, A_n is greater than 0 only when a seller who owns and uses the dwelling moves to the rental market. In other cases, A_n is equal to 0.

2. The WTP value can be expressed by the following general formula:

$$WTP = V + A_p \tag{3}$$

where V is a buyer's/tenant's self-valuation taken as the property's market price (P_m) for the sales market or market rent (R_m) for the rental market, A_p is an adjustment due to the price reference point being the expected price (P_e) or expected rent (R_e). For a buyer when $P_e < P_m$ (down market) then $(P_e - P_m) < A_p < 0$; otherwise 0 (up market). An analogous situation exists in the rental market. The value of WTP does not depend on A_o and A_l, since the reference points for buyers and tenants are, respectively, the lack of ownership/possession of the dwelling as well as the lack of attachment to the location and neighbourhood in which it is located. Therefore, the purchase of a dwelling resulting in the inclusion of its ownership and location in the buyer's/tenant's endowment will be treated by him/her as a gain not requiring additional compensation. Ultimately, the element A_n is not included in Equation (3) because, as indicated earlier, it relates to sellers.

3. A housing good can be either an exchange or consumption for sellers/landlords and buyers/tenants. In the primary sales market, a housing good is only exchanged in nature for a seller because the latter has not used it and wants to earn income from its sale. In the secondary sales market, for the seller, the housing good can be both exchanged (e.g. previously purchased as a form of investment) and consumption in nature (until the transaction, it served as a good to satisfy housing needs). Buyers making transactions may do so for investment purposes (an exchange good) or for housing purposes (a consumer good), regardless of the sales segment of the housing market. Ultimately, the situation in rental markets is analogous to that in sales markets, except that landlords are on the supply side and tenants are on the demand side of the market.

It should be emphasised that the conceptual formulas (2) and (3) for the value of WTA and WTP fit within the framework of the new behavioural economics, which calls for the extension of existing neoclassical models to include behavioural phenomena (Kahneman, 2003), rather than their complete replacement as in the old behavioural economics (Sent, 2004). In the context of house price modelling, the basic tool of mainstream economics is the Rosen (1974) hedonic model, as highlighted in the Introduction of this monograph as well as in Section 2.1.2. This model is used to determine market prices of properties by means of their utility-bearing characteristics. In formulas (2) and (3), this approach is de facto included under the designation V, which stands for the market price of the property. Consequently, the grounds for the parties to the transaction to determine the bid or offer prices lie in neoclassical economics. Only then does the process of adjusting the values of the WTA and WTP by the individuals take place following the tendency of reference dependence. On this basis, another extremely interesting conclusion can be drawn. Namely, the process of forming WTA and WTP values is similar to the mode of operation of anchoring and adjustment heuristic. The initial estimate, i.e. the anchor for WTA and WTP is V while the elements $A_p + A_o + A_l + A_n$ serve as adjustments. Ultimately, this all leads to the cognitive bias that is the endowment effect.

Table 2.1 presents the WTA and WTP values for sellers/landlords and buyers/tenats for primary and secondary markets, broken down by sales and rental markets and taking into account the nature of the housing good (exchangeable/consumable). Table 2.1 presents the most typical housing market transactions. More complicated situations, e.g. where the seller changes the form of housing tenure, were not analysed,[4] and therefore considerations of the size of A_n were omitted from the table.

Table 2.2 shows the calculated differences between the WTA and WTP based on Table 2.1. In each case, the difference is greater than 0, which means that the endowment effect occurs in primary and secondary sales and rental housing markets during both rising and falling prices independently of how the parties to the transaction treat the housing good (exchange/consumption good).

Based on theoretical considerations, it is also possible to identify variations in the strength of the endowment effect across housing market segments. First, the reference price theory analysis performed in Section 2.2.1 and to date housing studies suggest that, in general, the price adjustments of sellers/landlords will be higher than those of buyers/tenants, i.e. $A_p^{s..} > \left| A_p^{b..} \right|$, with the former occurring during up market. Based on this and the information in Table 2.2, it can be concluded that the endowment effect may be stronger during an upward price trend in the housing market.

Table 2.2 also presents that the endowment effect will be greater in the secondary market than in the primary market, regardless of whether it is a sales or rental market, because only within the secondary market are there transactions where the seller/landlord is the consumer of the transacted good which increases the strength of the endowment effect by the adjustments resulting from the ownership/possession and locational reference points – the loss of ownership/possession of the dwelling and its associated neighbourhood and location.

Table 2.1 WTA and WTP for sellers/landlords and buyers/tenants in the housing market in theory.

Party	Market segment	Good nature	Initial self-valuation	Reference price	Final reference price	Price adjustment (A_p)	Ownership/possession adjustment (A_o)	Locational adjustment (A_l)	WTA and WTP
Seller	Primary sales market	Exchange good	Market price (P_m)	Construction cost and land price (P_c); alternative transaction price (P_a); expected price (P_e)	P_e	If $P_m < P_e$ then $(P_e - P_m) > A_p^{s,e,s} > 0$; otherwise $A_p^{s,e,s} = 0$	$A_o^s = 0$ because exchange good	$A_l^s = 0$ because exchange good	$WTA = P_m + A_p^{s,e,s}$ if $P_m < P_e$ (up market); $WTA = P_m$ if $P_m > P_e$ (down market)
Seller	Secondary sales market	Exchange good	Market price (P_m)	Initial purchase price (P_o); intermediate price (P_n); alternative transaction price (P_a); expected price (P_e)	P_e	If $P_m < P_e$ then $(P_e - P_m) > A_p^{s,e,s} > 0$; otherwise $A_p^{s,e,s} = 0$	$A_o^s = 0$ because exchange good	$A_l^s = 0$ because exchange good	$WTA = P_m + A_p^{s,e,s}$ if $P_m < P_e$ (up market); $WTA = P_m$ if $P_m > P_e$ (down market)
Seller	Secondary market	Consumption good	Market price (P_m)	Initial purchase price (P_o); intermediate price (P_n); alternative transaction price (P_a); expected price (P_e)	P_e	If $P_m < P_e$ then $(P_e - P_m) > A_p^{s,c,s} > 0$; otherwise $A_p^{s,c,s} = 0$	$A_o^s > 0$ because consumption good	$A_l^s > 0$ because consumption good	$WTA = P_m + A_p^{s,c,s} + A_o^s + A_l^s$ if $P_m < P_e$ (up market); $WTA = P_m + A_o^s + A_l^s$ if $P_m > P_e$ (down market)
Buyer	Primary sales market	Exchange good	Market price (P_m)	Alternative bid price (P_a); expected price (P_e)	P_e	If $P_m > P_e$ then $(P_e - P_m) < A_p^{b,e,s} < 0$; otherwise $A_p^{b,e,s} = 0$	$A_o^s = 0$ because buyer	$A_l^s = 0$ because buyer	$WTP = P_m$ if $P_m < P_e$ (up market); $WTP = P_m - A_p^{b,e,s}$ if $P_m > P_e$ (down market)

(Continued)

Party	Market segment	Good nature	Initial self-valuation	Reference price	Final reference price	Price adjustment (A_p)	Ownership/possession adjustment (A_o)	Locational adjustment (A_l)	WTA and WTP
Buyer	Primary sales market	Consumption good	Market price (P_m)	Alternative bid price (P_a); expected price (P_e)	P_e	If $P_m > P_e$, then $(P_e - P_m) < A_p^{b,c,s} < 0$; otherwise $A_p^{b,c,s} = 0$	$A_o^s = 0$ because buyer	$A_l^s = 0$ because buyer	$WTP = P_m$ if $P_m < P_e$ (up market); $WTP = P_m - A_p^{b,c,s}$ if $P_m > P_e$ (down market)
Buyer	Secondary sales market	Exchange good	Market price (P_m)	Alternative bid price (P_a); expected price (P_e)	P_e	If $P_m > P_e$ then $(P_e - P_m) < A_p^{b,e,s} < 0$; otherwise $A_p^{b,e,s} = 0$	$A_o^s = 0$ because buyer	$A_l^s = 0$ because buyer	$WTP = P_m$ if $P_m < P_e$ (up market); $WTP = P_m - A_p^{b,e,s}$ if $P_m > P_e$ (down market)
Buyer	Secondary sales market	Consumption good	Market price (P_m)	Alternative bid price (P_a); expected price (P_e)	P_e	If $P_m > P_e$, then $(P_e - P_m) < A_p^{b,c,s} < 0$; otherwise $A_p^{b,c,s} = 0$	$A_o^s = 0$ because buyer	$A_l^s = 0$ because buyer	$WTP = P_m$ if $P_m < P_e$ (up market); $WTP = P_m - A_p^{b,c,s}$ if $P_m > P_e$ (down market)
Landlord	Primary rental market	Exchange good	Market rent (R_m)	Construction cost and land price (P_c); alternative transaction rent (R_a); expected rent (R_e)	R_e	If $R_m < R_e$, then $(R_e - R_m) > A_p^{s,e,r} > 0$; otherwise $A_p^{s,e,r} = 0$	$A_o^r = 0$ because exchange good	$A_l^r = 0$ because exchange good	$WTA = R_m + A_p^{s,e,r}$ if $R_m < R_e$ (up market); $WTA = R_m$ if $R_m > R_e$ (down market)
Landlord	Secondary rental market	Exchange good	Market rent (R_m)	Initial purchase price (P_o); intermediate rent (R_n); alternative transaction rent (R_a); expected rent (R_e)	R_e	If $R_m < R_e$, then $(R_e - R_m) > A_p^{s,e,r} > 0$; otherwise $A_p^{s,e,r} = 0$	$A_o^r = 0$ because exchange good	$A_l^r = 0$ because exchange good	$WTA = R_m + A_p^{s,e,r}$ if $R_m < R_e$ (up market); $WTA = R_m$ if $R_m > R_e$ (down market)

(Continued)

Table 2.1 (Continued)

Party	Market segment	Good nature	Initial self-valuation	Reference price	Final reference price	Price adjustment (A_p)	Ownership/possession adjustment (A_o)	Locational adjustment (A_l)	WTA and WTP
Land-lord	Secondary rental market	Consumption good	Market rent (R_m)	Initial purchase price (P_o); intermediate rent (R_{in}); alternative transaction rent (R_a); expected rent (R_e)	R_e	If $R_m < R_e$ then $(R_e - R_m) > A_p^{s,c,r} > 0$; otherwise $A_p^{s,c,r} = 0$	$A_o^r > 0$ because consumption good	$A_l^r > 0$ because consumption good	$WTA = R_m + A_p^{s,c,r} + A_o^r + A_l^r$ if $R_m < R_e$ (up market); $WTA = R_m + A_o^r + A_l^r$ if $R_m > R_e$ (down market)
Tenant	Primary rental market	Exchange good	Market rent (R_m)	Alternative bid rent (R_a); expected rent (R_e)	R_e	If $R_m > R_e$ then $(R_e - R_m) < A_p^{b,e,r} < 0$; otherwise $A_p^{b,e,r} = 0$	$A_o^r = 0$ because buyer-tenant	$A_l^r = 0$ because buyer-tenant	$WTP = R_m$ if $R_m < R_e$ (up market); $WTP = R_m - A_p^{b,e,r}$ if $R_m > R_e$ (down market)
Tenant	Primary rental market	Consumption good	Market rent (R_m)	Alternative bid rent (R_a); expected rent (R_e)	R_e	If $R_m > R_e$ then $(R_e - R_m) < A_p^{b,c,r} < 0$; otherwise $A_p^{b,c,r} = 0$	$A_o^r = 0$ because buyer-tenant	$A_l^r = 0$ because buyer-tenant	$WTP = R_m$ if $R_m < R_e$ (up market); $WTP = R_m - A_p^{b,c,r}$ if $R_m > R_e$ (down market)
Tenant	Secondary rental market	Exchange good	Market rent (R_m)	Alternative bid rent (R_a); expected rent (R_e)	R_e	If $R_m > R_e$ then $(R_e - R_m) < A_p^{b,e,r} < 0$; otherwise $A_p^{b,e,r} = 0$	$A_o^r = 0$ because buyer-tenant	$A_l^r = 0$ because buyer-tenant	$WTP = R_m$ if $R_m < R_e$ (up market); $WTP = R_m - A_p^{b,e,r}$ if $R_m > R_e$ (down market)
Tenant	Secondary rental market	Consumption good	Market rent (R_m)	Alternative bid rent (R_a); expected rent (R_e)	R_e	If $R_m > R_e$ then $(R_e - R_m) < A_p^{b,c,r} < 0$; otherwise $A_p^{b,c,r} = 0$	$A_o^r = 0$ because buyer-tenant	$A_l^r = 0$ because buyer-tenant	$WTP = R_m$ if $R_m < R_e$ (up market); $WTP = R_m - A_p^{b,c,r}$ if $R_m > R_e$ (down market)

Source: Own study.

Note: A_l has three superscripts. First: s – seller/landlord; b – buyer/tenant. Second: e – exchange good; c – consumption good. Third: s – sales market

Table 2.2 The difference between WTA and WTP in housing markets in theory.

Sales housing market		Seller-PE	Seller-SE	Seller-SC
Buyer-PE	Up market	$A_p^{s,e,s}$	–	–
	Down market	$\left|A_p^{b,e,s}\right|$	–	–
Buyer-PC	Up market	$A_p^{s,e,s}$	–	–
	Down market	$\left|A_p^{b,c,s}\right|$	–	–
Buyer-SE	Up market	–	$A_p^{s,e,s}$	$A_p^{s,c,s}+A_o^s+A_l^s$
	Down market	–	$\left|A_p^{b,e,s}\right|$	$\left|A_p^{b,e,s}\right|+A_o^s+A_l^s$
Buyer-SC	Up market	–	$A_p^{s,e,s}$	$A_p^{s,c,s}+A_o^s+A_l^s$
	Down market	–	$\left|A_p^{b,c,s}\right|$	$\left|A_p^{b,c,s}\right|+A_o^s+A_l^s$
Rental housing market		**Landlord-PE**	**Landlord-SE**	**Landlord-SC**
Tenant-PE	Up market	$A_p^{s,e,r}$	–	–
	Down market	$\left|A_p^{b,e,r}\right|$	–	–
Tenant-PC	Up market	$A_p^{s,e,r}$	–	–
	Down market	$\left|A_p^{b,c,r}\right|$	–	–
Tenant-SE	Up market	–	$A_p^{s,e,r}$	$A_p^{s,c,r}+A_o^r+A_l^r$
	Down market	–	$\left|A_p^{b,e,r}\right|$	$\left|A_p^{b,e,r}\right|+A_o^r+A_l^r$
Tenant-SC	Up market	–	$A_p^{s,e,r}$	$A_p^{s,c,r}+A_o^r+A_l^r$
	Down market	–	$\left|A_p^{b,c,r}\right|$	$\left|A_p^{b,c,r}\right|+A_o^r+A_l^r$

Source: Own study.

Note: P represents the primary market. S represents the secondary market. E represents the exchange good. C represents the consumption good.

Finally, in Section 2.2.1, disutility from transactions in terms of the ownership/possession reference point will be greater for the seller in the secondary sales housing market than for the landlord in the secondary rental housing market, because the seller gives away legal ownership and possession of the property and the landlord only possession (in the case of housing transactions where sellers/landlords treat dwellings as a consumer good). Assuming that in relative terms the price adjustments to self-valuations made by transaction parties in the sales and rental markets will be similar, then the percentage endowment effect will be greater in the secondary sales housing market, i.e. $\dfrac{A_p^{.s} + A_o^s + A_l^s}{P_m} > \dfrac{A_p^{.r} + A_o^r + A_l^r}{R_m}$. This automatically implies that the endowment effect in the secondary sales housing market is stronger than that in the primary rental housing market.

2.2.3   Additional considerations

The sublease housing market

There is also a sublease market in the housing market where a tenant rents a dwelling to another person. In this market, the endowment effect may also occur because sublandlords shaping the WTA value refer to the price reference point as well as to the ownership/possession reference point. The latter reference point will apply only to those sublandlords who previously used the dwelling, and therefore the loss of possession may involve a demand for some compensation. However, Lewicka (2010) pointed out that attachment to the home is less for tenants who are not owners. Ultimately, it can be assumed that the endowment effect in the sublease market is weaker than that in the sales and rental markets.

Changing the form of housing tenure from ownership to tenancy

As indicated earlier, the endowment effect can be amplified for the seller who is the consumer of the transacted dwelling if he or she goes from the sales market to the rental market. This situation is particularly noticeable when ownership is regarded by the public as the right form of housing tenure. Consequently, its loss can be extremely painful and cause a significant increase in the value of the WTA.

Buying rented dwellings

In the housing market, there are sometimes situations in which an existing tenant wants to buy ownership of a rented dwelling. For this type of transaction, the endowment effect can be significantly reduced or reversed. For example, during an up market, the seller's WTA is equal to $WTA=P_m+A_p$, while the WTP value of the existing tenant will be equal to $WTP=P_m+A_o+A_l$. The value of WTP is increased by the components of A_o+A_l, because there is a probability that the tenant has introduced the rented dwelling into his/her endowment (the fact of possession and attachment to the neighbourhood and location) and therefore, the situation of not buying out the dwelling will treat as a loss. In this case, the WTA-WTP gap will be: $A_p-A_o-A_l$, which may even imply a reverse endowment effect when $A_p<(A_o+A_l)$.

The role of real estate agents

The considerations presented in this section do not take into account the participation of real estate agents during housing market transactions. Their impact on the size of the endowment effect may be twofold. First, as a result of agents' involvement, the WTA-WTP gap may narrow due to agents' attempts to rationalise the price expectations of buyers/tenants as well as sellers/landlords. Agents are experts and possess a significant amount of information about the housing market. One of their tasks is to advise the parties to the transaction on a fair bid or offer price (Bernheim & Meer, 2013). On the other hand, agents charge the parties to the transaction a commission that is usually a fixed percentage of the final transaction price. The need to pay the commission may be framed by the parties to the transaction as a loss requiring compensation, which may result in an increase in WTA and a decrease in WTP. Therefore, it is ad hoc impossible to determine clearly how real estate agents can affect the size of the endowment effect in the housing market. However, in Poland, having to pay a commission has an unambiguously negative connotation in most cases (Ostrowska, 2014), which encourages the interpretation that the participation of a real estate agent in a transaction may lead to an intensification of the endowment effect.

Buyers' attachment to location

Equation 3 does not include the A_l element because, in general, buyers/tenants are not attached to the specific locations where the dwellings they are acquiring are situated. However, in extreme situations there may be transactions where, even before the transaction, buyers'/tenants' endowments include the locations of the dwellings being transacted. This may include situations where a household decides to buy/rent a larger flat in the same location, e.g. in the same block of flats or the immediate vicinity. In this case, the fact of not purchasing/renting a dwelling in a location the buyers/tenants desire will be treated as a loss, resulting in their WTP value being increased by the A_l element, which should lead to a narrowing of the WTA-WTP gap.

2.3 Summary

Based on these theoretical considerations, it is possible to answer the research questions posed in Chapter 2.

RQ4. From a theoretical perspective, what are the reference points in housing transactions and how do they affect the formation of the endowment effect in the housing market?

The theoretical considerations presented in this chapter indicate that each buyer, seller, and their counterparts in the rental market have a price reference point. This point is variable and depends on the amount of information held by the party in the transaction. Ultimately, however, it appears that the final price reference point for a housing transaction is the expected price of the property in the sales market and the expected rent in the rental market. Following this reference point during the up market, sellers/landlords increase their self-valuations. Buyers/tenants, on the other hand, will lower their self-valuations during the downward market. Furthermore, for sellers/landlords who have consumed (lived in) the property being sold/rented, two more reference points are also important: the ownership/possession reference point and the locational reference point. These types of sellers/landlords have a strong attachment to their dwellings and their associated neighbourhood and location, which means that the loss of these elements from their endowments will necessitate elevated compensation. This compensation will be relatively lower in the rental market, where the landlord loses possession while retaining legal ownership of the property. Finally, the last reference point relates to social norms and, in particular, to the right form of housing tenure. However, this point is only in play when a household changes the form of housing tenure from ownership to tenancy, assuming that for society, the former form is the only appropriate one. In such a case, the seller's WTA value may further increase.

RQ5. According to the theory, does the strength of endowment effects differ between sales and rental markets and across primary and secondary markets?

Table 2.2 shows that the strength of the endowment effects changes between the sales and rental housing markets as well as between the primary and secondary markets. First, the endowment effect is stronger in secondary markets than in primary markets, regardless of whether the sales or rental markets are analysed. This is because only in secondary markets there are transactions where sellers/landlords treated dwellings as consumer goods which increases the endowment effect due to the activation of the ownership/possession and locational reference points. Further, it is predicted that a significant difference in the relative strength of the endowment effect will occur between the sales and rental markets because the seller in the sales market gives away ownership and possession of the dwelling, whereas in the rental market the landlord only transfers possession.

Notes

1 Researchers have pointed out several other characteristics of real estate. For example, Kucharska-Stasiak (2006) mentions that real estate has physical characteristics such as complexity, fixity in place, permanence, heterogeneity, and indivisibility; economic characteristics such as rarity, location, interdependence, capital intensity, and low liquidity; and institutional-legal characteristics such as real estate rights and institutional features.
2 Several theoretical and empirical studies assume that the basis for estimating the value of a property by the parties to a transaction is its market value. For example, Dittmann (2014) pointed to this fact when analysing the behaviour of real estate developers.
3 Sprenger (2015) explains that the endowment effect for risk should be distinguished from the endowment effect where the referent is fixed. In the latter case, the endowment effect is the WTA-WTP gap, while in the former it should be understood as a risk preference mismatch between risk-taking when the reference point is fixed and

risk-taking when it is stochastic. Taking a fixed value of the price reference point derived from expectations does not mean that the assumption that the housing market is risky is rejected, since the expected price may be the product of considering several different scenarios characterised by certain probabilities. In addition, housing literature examines the house price expectations of individuals as fixed values (see, for example, Hjalmarsson and Österholm (2020)).
4 Głuszak (2015) empirically proved that the transition from the sales market to the rental market is extremely rare.

References

Adair, A. S., Berry, J. N., & McGreal, W. S. (1996). Hedonic modelling, housing submarkets and residential valuation. *Journal of Property Research*, *13*(1), 67–83. https://doi.org/10.1080/095999196368899

Bao, H. X., & Gong, C. M. (2016). Endowment effect and housing decisions. *International Journal of Strategic Property Management*, *20*(4), 341–353. https://doi.org/10.3846/1648715X.2016.1192069

Bao, H. X., & Saunders, R. (2023). Reference dependence in the UK housing market. *Housing Studies*, *38*(7), 1191–1219. https://doi.org /10.1080/02673037.2021.1935767

Bernheim, B. D., & Meer, J. (2013). Do real estate brokers add value when listing services are unbundled? *Economic Inquiry*, *51*(2), 1166–1182. https://doi.org/10.1111/j.1465-7295.2012.00473.x

Boelhouwer, P. (2011). Neo-classical economic theory on housing markets and behavioural sciences: Ally or opponent? *Housing, Theory and Society*, *28*(3), 276–280. https://doi.org/10.1080/14036096 .2011.599173

Clayton, J. (1998). Further evidence on real estate market efficiency. *Journal of Real Estate Research*, *15*(1), 41–57. https://doi.org/10.10 80/10835547.1998.12090915

Cotteleer, G., Gardebroek, C., & Luijt, J. (2008). Market power in a GIS-based hedonic price model of local farmland markets. *Land Economics*, *84*(4), 573–592. https://doi.org/10.3368/le.84.4.573

Dittmann, I. (2014). Setting offer prices by housing developers-selected issues in the light of literature review. *Real Estate Management and Valuation*, *22*(4), 17–26. https://doi.org/10.2478/remav-2014-0033

Fallis, G. (1985). *Housing economics*. Butterworths.

Głuszak, M. (2015). Multinomial logit model of housing demand in Poland. *Real Estate Management and Valuation*, *23*(1), 84–89. https://doi.org/10.1515/remav-2015-0008

Głuszak, M., & Rymarzak, M. (2019). Expectations and house prices: An exploratory analysis. *World of Real Estate Journal*, *110*(4), 15–28. https://doi.org/10.14659/worej.2019.110.02

Gong, C. M., Lizieri, C., & Bao, H. X. (2019). "Smarter information, smarter consumers"? Insights into the housing market. *Journal of Business Research, 97*, 51–64. https://doi.org/10.1016/j.jbusres.2018. 12.036

Goodman, A. C. (1983). Willingness to pay for car efficiency: A hedonic price approach. *Journal of Transport Economics and Policy*, 247–266.

Green, R. K., & Malpezzi, S. (2003). *A primer on US housing markets and housing policy*. The Urban Institute.

Hidalgo, M. C., & Hernandez, B. (2001). Place attachment: Conceptual and empirical questions. *Journal of Environmental Psychology, 21*(3), 273–281. https://doi.org/10.1006/jevp.2001.0221

Hjalmarsson, E., & Österholm, P. (2020). Heterogeneity in households' expectations of housing prices–evidence from micro data. *Journal of Housing Economics, 50*, 101731. https://doi.org/10.1016/j. jhe.2020.101731

Kahneman, D. (2003). Maps of bounded rationality: Psychology for behavioral economics. *American Economic Review, 93*(5), 1449–1475. https://doi.org/10.1257/000282803322655392

Kucharska-Stasiak, E. (2006). *Nieruchomość a rynek*. Wydawnictwo Naukowe PWN.

Kuchler, T., Piazzesi, M., & Stroebel, J. (2023). Housing market expectations. In R. Bachmann, G. Topa, & W. van der Klaauw (Eds.), *Handbook of economic expectations* (pp. 163–191). Academic Press.

Levy, D., Murphy, L., & Lee, C. K. C. (2008). Influences and emotions: Exploring family decision-making processes when buying a house. *Housing Studies, 23*(2), 271–289. https://doi.org/10.1080/ 02673030801893164

Lewicka, M. (2010). What makes neighborhood different from home and city? Effects of place scale on place attachment. *Journal of Environmental Psychology, 30*(1), 35–51. https://doi.org/10.1016/j. jenvp.2009.05.004

Lux, M., Gibas, P., Boumová, I., Hájek, M., & Sunega, P. (2017). Reasoning behind choices: Rationality and social norms in the housing market behaviour of first-time buyers in the Czech Republic. *Housing Studies, 32*(4), 517–539. https://doi.org/10.1080/02673037.2016.1219331

Lux, M., & Sunega, P. (2022). Pragmatic socioeconomics: A way towards new findings on sources of (housing) market instability. *Housing, Theory and Society, 39*(2), 129–146. https://doi.org/10.1 080/14036096.2020.1853226

Lux, M., Sunega, P., & Jakubek, J. (2020). Impact of weak substitution between owning and renting a dwelling on housing market. *Journal of Housing and the Built Environment, 35*, 1–25. https://doi. org/10.1007/s10901-019-09661-3

Malpezzi, S. (2003). Hedonic pricing models: A selective and applied review. In T. O'Sullivan & K. Gibb (Eds.), *Housing economics and public policy* (pp. 67–89). Wiley. https://doi.org/10.1002/9780470690680.ch5

Morrison, P. S., & Clark, W. A. (2016). Loss aversion and duration of residence. *Demographic Research, 35*, 1079–1100. https://doi.org/10.4054/DemRes.2016.35.36

Olsen, E. O. (1969). A competitive theory of the housing market. *American Economic Review, 59*, 612–622.

Ostrowska, I. (2014). Analiza zalet i wad korzystania z usług pośrednictwa w obrocie nieruchomościami na podstawie opinii konsumentów. *Marketing i Zarządzanie, 34*, 161–171.

Oxley, M. J., & Haffner, M. E. A. (2012). Comparative housing research. In S. J. Smith, M. Elsinga, L. Fox O'Mahony, O. Seow Eng, S. Wachter, & K. Gibb (Eds.), *International encyclopedia of housing and home* (Vol. 12, pp. 199–209). Elsevier.

Reb, J., & Connolly, T. (2007). Possession, feelings of ownership and the endowment effect. *Judgment and Decision Making, 2*(2), 107–114. https://doi.org/10.1017/S1930297500000085

Rosen, S. (1974). Hedonic prices and implicit markets: Product differentiation in pure competition. *Journal of Political Economy, 82*(1), 34–55. https://doi.org/10.1086/260169

Sent, E. M. (2004). Behavioral economics: How psychology made its (limited) way back into economics. *History of Political Economy, 36*(4), 735–760. https://doi.org/10.1215/00182702-36-4-735

Shu, S. B., & Peck, J. (2011). Psychological ownership and affective reaction: Emotional attachment process variables and the endowment effect. *Journal of Consumer Psychology, 21*(4), 439–452. https://doi.org/10.1016/j.jcps.2011.01.002

Smith, S. J. (2011). Home price dynamics: A behavioural economy? *Housing, Theory and Society, 28*(3), 236–261. https://doi.org/10.1080/14036096.2011.599179

Sprenger, C. (2015). An endowment effect for risk: Experimental tests of stochastic reference points. *Journal of Political Economy, 123*(6), 1456–1499. https://doi.org/10.1086/683836

Weaver, R., & Frederick, S. (2012). A reference price theory of the endowment effect. *Journal of Marketing Research, 49*(5), 696–707. https://doi.org/10.1509/jmr.09.0103

Wen, H., Chu, L., Zhang, J., & Xiao, Y. (2018). Competitive intensity, developer expectation, and land price: Evidence from Hangzhou, China. *Journal of Urban Planning and Development, 144*(4), 04018040. https://doi.org/10.1061/(ASCE)UP.1943-5444.0000490

Yan, J., & Bao, H. X. (2018). A prospect theory-based analysis of housing satisfaction with relocations: Field evidence from China. *Cities, 83*, 193–202. https://doi.org/10.1016/j.cities.2018.06.022

3 Endowment effects and the Polish housing market

A case study

Chapter overview

This chapter aims to assess the presence of endowment effects in sales and rental housing markets in Poland, taking into account the theoretical predictions conceptualised in Chapter 2. The chapter starts with a presentation of the specifics of the Polish housing market, including data on (i) price levels, (ii) the size of sales and rental markets distinguishing between primary and secondary markets, and (iii) housing affordability. This is intended to provide the reader with the context of the Polish housing market against other markets. A lab-in-the-field experiment is used to obtain data and the contingent valuation method (CVM) is employed to elicit WTA (willingness to accept) and WTP (willingness to pay) values. Groups of Polish homeowners and renters participated in the experiment, with a division into sellers/landlords and buyers/tenants. The findings suggest that the endowment effect significantly shapes the housing market in Poland, with its strength varying across its different segments. In summary, this chapter answers the following research question.

RQ6. Is there an endowment effect on the Polish housing market? If so, does the magnitude of the endowment effect differ between sales and rental markets, and across primary and secondary markets?

3.1 Characteristics of the Polish housing market

3.1.1 Housing statistics

Polish households mostly meet their housing needs by living in houses (see Figure 3.1a). Specifically, in 2022, 58.2% of Polish households

DOI: 10.1201/9781003512004-4

resided in houses, and 41.8% resided in flats. These results do not stand out from the European Union average, in contrast to the housing tenure preferences. In Poland, the homeownership rate has been increasing over the years, reaching nearly 90% by 2022 (see Figure 3.1b). Renting, especially renting at the market rate, is very unpopular; in 2022, only 3.4% of households rent a dwelling on the private market to meet their housing needs.

The dominance of ownership over renting in Poland, but also in other Central and Eastern European (CEE) countries, is due to several reasons. First, after 1990, following the transformation of the economies of these countries from socialist to market type, new democratic governments massively privatised public housing stock through the ability to purchase housing at low prices (Lux & Sunega, 2014). Second, there is no political environment in CEE countries that supports forms of housing tenure other than ownership (Hegedüs et al., 2018). Rubaszek and Czerniak (2017) point to several other reasons for the development of homeownership rate in Poland, including low interest rates, regulations limiting the supply of rental housing, such as excessive protection for tenants, and the lack of clear regulations on maximum rent changes. This has led to a situation in which Poland and other CEE countries have a housing regime called super-homeownership. Lux and Sugena (2020) note that such a regime generates positive as well as negative outcomes. The former includes providing households with a sense of security and freedom. Being a homeowner increases the household's wealth and enables it to reap capital gains. On the other hand, a super-homeownership regime may intensify the problem of housing affordability in the younger part of the population. Under this system, a large proportion of the population is trapped in low-quality housing. Further, a housing system with dominant ownership is more susceptible to economic shocks affecting housing prices. Finally, given the theoretical considerations outlined in Chapter 2, there may be high friction in the housing market based on super-homeownership due to the endowment effect, the strength of which is expected to be greater in the sales market than in the rental market.

Over the past decade, housing prices in Poland have been rising, as seen in Figure 3.2a, and the price increase is particularly noticeable after 2016. In general, the average transaction price of flats in Poland was higher in the primary market than in the secondary market. However, in recent years, a strong price convergence process has occurred between these markets. In 2010, the difference between the average

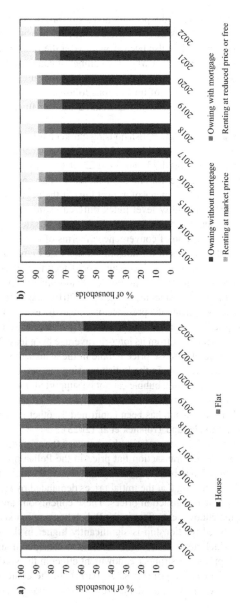

Figure 3.1 a) The structure of residential property type in Poland; b) The structure of housing tenure in Poland.

Source: Own study based on data from https://ec.europa.eu/eurostat.

flat price per square meter in the primary and secondary markets was EUR 301, and in 2022, it was EUR 108. The number of transactions in the Polish housing market has also been growing over the years, and its highest level was reached in 2021 when the number of concluded sales contracts exceeded 240,000. In 2020, there was a noticeable decline in the dynamics of the number of transactions following the outbreak of the COVID-19 pandemic and the associated time of uncertainty (Tomal, 2023b).

Dynamic price growth in the Polish housing market has not reduced housing affordability, as measured by the house price-to-income (PTI) ratio. The latter in 2010 was 1.33, and in 2022, it was already 1.08, which meant that, on average, for one gross monthly salary, one could buy almost all of one square meter of a dwelling. At the beginning of 2010, the housing affordability level index differed significantly between primary and secondary markets. As in the case of sales prices, one can see the phenomenon of convergence in terms of PTI between the aforementioned segments of the housing market (see Figure 3.3a). The PTI is also a frequently used measure for detecting real estate bubbles, as it shows the undervaluation/overvaluation of the housing market compared to its fundamental value. Asal (2019) specified that a high PTI value may indicate the presence of unrealistic expectations for future house price increases. Bourassa et al. (2019) emphasised that a deviation of the current PTI from its long-run average by at least 20% indicates the presence of a house price bubble in the analysed period. As can be seen in Figure 3.3b, in the Polish housing market, the conclusion about the existence of a bubble cannot be supported, indicating that the price increases observed in recent years were based on market fundamentals. This conclusion has been confirmed by other researchers such as Tomal (2022a) and Trojanek et al. (2023).

Finally, Figure 3.4 shows the relationship between the average offer flat price and the average transaction flat price in the Polish housing market. This relationship in both the primary and secondary markets is greater than zero, indicating that the initial prices demanded by sellers are higher than the final transaction prices. These conclusions are the first to indicate the endowment effect in the Polish housing market. In addition, the analysed relationship is significantly higher in the secondary market, which also fits with the theoretical considerations in Chapter 2, which predicts a stronger endowment effect in the secondary sales market than in the primary sales market. In the context of the rental market, the only data available are for the secondary market

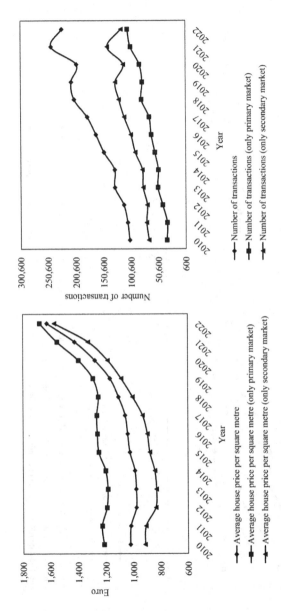

Figure 3.2 a) Average house price per square metre in the Polish housing market; b) The number of transactions in the Polish housing market.

Source: Own study based on data from https://bdl.stat.gov.pl/bdl/start.

Note: One Polish zloty (PLN) is equal to 4.4475 Euro on 31.10.2023. The data is for the flat market only.

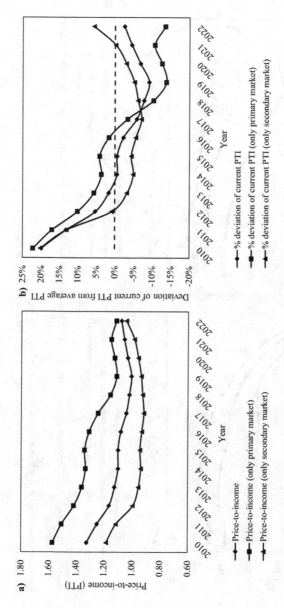

Figure 3.3 a) House price-to-income (PTI) ratio; b) % deviation of current PTI from historical average of PTI.

Source: Own study based on data from https://bdl.stat.gov.pl/bdl/start.

Note: The data is for the flat market only. PTI is defined as the relation between the average house price per square meter and the average gross monthly salary.

because the primary market for residential rentals is extremely under-developed in Poland and is only just beginning to take off in the country. Interestingly, the ratio of average offer rent to average transaction rent in the secondary rental market is quite variable but generally lies between the analogous ratios calculated for the secondary and primary sales markets. This is also in line with the theory that the endowment effect should be stronger in the secondary sales housing market than in the secondary rental housing market.

In conclusion, the Polish housing market is an important object of study in terms of the potential presence of the endowment effect. Because it operates under the regime of super-homeownership, the strong endowment effect in this market may significantly weaken its cleaning process, leading to its inefficiency. The results of this study should also be useful for other countries with a dominant form of ownership as housing tenure.

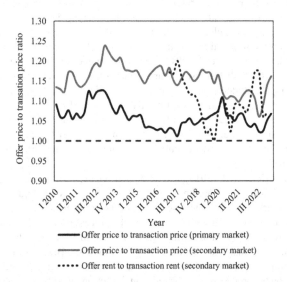

Figure 3.4 Relationship between the average offer price (rent) and average transaction price (rent).

Source: Own study based on data from https://nbp.pl/

Note: The data cover only the flat market in the seven largest Polish cities (Gdansk, Gdynia, Cracow, Lodz, Poznan, Wroclaw, and Warsaw). Gdynia and Lodz were omitted from the rental market due to missing data.

3.1.2   *Behavioural biases: a review*

The Polish housing market has been studied to identify behavioural biases. In particular, previous analyses have focused on the certainty effect, isolation effect, information cascade phenomenon, anchoring and adjustment heuristic, and loss aversion.

The certainty effect means that people tend to choose outcomes that are considered certain over those that are only probable (Kahneman & Tversky, 1979). Brzezicka et al. (2013) performed a laboratory experiment on a group of students and university employees in Olsztyn, Poland to verify the certainty effect. The experiment participants were asked to imagine that they were making a choice between a) purchasing a residential property having a certain price per square meter and b) purchasing a residential property having probabilities assigned to certain prices. As many as 82% of the respondents chose the certainty offer, with the proportion being lower for women (75%).

The isolation effect refers to the situation in which people make simplifications for similar alternatives when making decisions; that is, they focus on the elements that differentiate these alternatives, rather than on the probabilities of their occurrence (Kahneman & Tversky, 1979). Brzezicka et al. (2013) tested the incidence of the isolation effect in the Polish housing market with a laboratory experiment on a group of students and employees of a university in Olsztyn. Participants were asked to imagine that they owned a dwelling. They then made choices related to two problems: a) selling the dwelling to buy another better one and b) finding another better tenant. Finally, the isolation effect was confirmed only for the problem of property renting.

Brzezicka et al. (2015) also noted that prices of residential properties in Poland set in preliminary contracts are significantly higher than their market values. The researchers do not refer to the endowment effect in this case but rather argue that the process of price determination by non-professionals depends on the use of heuristics, that is, a set of individual and simplified ways of inference. Brzezicka (2016) attempted to identify the impact of anchoring and adjustment heuristic on the process of value creation in the housing market. This heuristic involves estimating an initial value (anchor) and then adjusting it to obtain a final value (Tversky & Kahneman, 1974). The results of a study on a group of university students in Olsztyn and Kielce showed that participants in the experiment anchored their self-valuations of properties to the prices given to them rather than to actual prices. Kokot (2023) also tested the existence of an anchoring effect in the Polish housing market. The results indicate that much of the price volatility in the market can be attributed to behavioural elements. Specifically, market participants are anchored on prices commonly considered typical, but not necessarily justified by market fundamentals.

Brzezicka (2014) and Brzezicka et al. (2018) also confirmed the existence of the information cascade phenomenon in the Polish housing market, that is, the tendency to make decisions based on observations of the behaviour of other members in a given group.

Further, Brzezicka and Tomal (2023) identified the phenomenon of loss aversion in the Polish housing market which is the underlying cause of the endowment effect. Specifically, the researchers performed an online experiment on a group of 203 respondents aged 25–40 in Warsaw with a university education. The results indicated that for housing goods, the average loss aversion coefficient was equal to 1.36, while for monetary goods, it was only 1.16.

In turn, Brzezicka and Wisniewski (2013) on a group of university students in Kielce and Olsztyn examined the importance of behavioural elements of the housing market for its participants. The latter includes both risk and uncertainty. The results indicated that 75% of respondents linked the real estate market directly with its strictly economic aspects, that is, price, buying, and selling, while 13% pointed to behavioural elements and 10% to psychological elements. A similar study was conducted by Rubaszek and Czerniak (2017), who found that several behavioural factors (e.g. peace of mind, and improved well-being) influence a household's preference for a form of housing tenure.

Finally, Tomal (2022b, 2023a), while analysing the accuracy of self-reported home valuations in the Warsaw housing market, found that the fraction of interviewees overestimating their properties ranged from 18% to 42% depending on the size of the margin of error adopted. These results may indicate that, at least in part, in the Polish population, the endowment effect may play a significant role in the decision-making process in the housing market.

The literature review presented here provides additional evidence that the Polish housing market is characterised by the occurrence of various behavioural biases that reduce its efficiency. However, to date, no study has investigated whether there is an endowment effect in this market.

3.2   Endowment effect identification: research results

3.2.1   Hypothesis tested

To answer research question RQ6, the predictions in terms of the strength of the endowment effect derived from the theoretical model described in Section 2.2.2 were concretised in the form of six research hypotheses:

H1. The endowment effect is present in the primary and secondary sales housing markets.

H2. The endowment effect is present in the primary and secondary rental housing markets.

H3. On average, the endowment effect is stronger during an upward house price trend.

H4. On average, the endowment effect is weaker in the primary sales housing market than in the secondary sales housing market.

H5. On average, the endowment effect is weaker in the primary rental housing market than in the secondary rental housing market.

H6. On average, the endowment effect is stronger in the sales housing market than in the rental housing market.

As seen in Table 2.2, the endowment effects should be the same in primary and secondary markets when the seller/landlord treats the housing good as an exchange good. This fact makes it possible to simplify the research procedure and reduces the research sample. In particular, the endowment effect in such a case will only depend on whether the market is in a period of growth or decline, the nature of the housing good being traded (exchangeable/consumable), and the market segment being analysed by sales and rental markets only (see Table 3.1). Taking this perspective, the WTA-WTP gap in the case of transactions in which the seller/landlord treats the housing good as an exchange good corresponds to transactions in the entire primary housing market and part of the secondary housing market. However, when the seller/landlord treats the housing good as a consumer good, the market segment studied is part of the secondary housing market.

Table 3.1 The difference between WTA and WTP in housing markets in simplified theory.

Sales housing market		Seller-exchange	Seller-consumption
Buyer-exchange	Up market	$A_p^{s,e,s}$	$A_p^{s,c,s} + A_o^s + A_l^s$
	Down market	$\left\| A_p^{b,e,s} \right\|$	$\left\| A_p^{b,e,s} \right\| + A_o^s + A_l^s$
Buyer-consumption	Up market	$A_p^{s,e,s}$	$A_p^{s,c,s} + A_o^s + A_l^s$
	Down market	$\left\| A_p^{b,c,s} \right\|$	$\left\| A_p^{b,c,s} \right\| + A_o^s + A_l^s$
Rental housing market		Landlord-exchange	Landlord-consumption
Tenant-exchange	Up market	$A_p^{s,e,r}$	$A_p^{s,c,r} + A_o^r + A_l^r$
	Down market	$\left\| A_p^{b,e,r} \right\|$	$\left\| A_p^{b,e,r} \right\| + A_o^r + A_l^r$
Tenant-consumption	Up market	$A_p^{s,e,r}$	$A_p^{s,c,r} + A_o^r + A_l^r$
	Down market	$\left\| A_p^{b,c,r} \right\|$	$\left\| A_p^{b,c,r} \right\| + A_o^r + A_l^r$

Source: Own study.

3.2.2 Experiment design

Data collection

To collect data on WTA and WTP values among participants of the Polish housing market, a lab-in-the-field experiment was used, the advantages of which are presented in Chapter 1, in the context of the phenomenon under analysis. Specifically, the experiment was performed outside a single laboratory, while its respondents answered subsequent questions in their unchanging environment, sitting in front of the same computer. The former characteristic is responsible for the "field" part and the latter for the "lab" part of the lab-in-the-field experiment design.

In the experiment, respondents generally acted either as sellers/landlords or as buyers/tenants of residential property. Respondents were recruited from actual property owners and real renters to increase the reliability of the results obtained. Four groups of respondents were randomly selected from the former population: (i) sellers and land-lords of housing as exchange goods, (ii) sellers and landlords of housing as consumer goods, (iii) buyers of housing as exchange goods, and (iv) buyers of housing as consumer goods. Meanwhile, among the tenant population, two groups were identified: (i) renters of housing as exchange goods and (ii) renters of housing as consumer goods.

An online panel data platform (OPDP) from *Prolific* (www.prolific. com/) was used to recruit the respondents. Palan and Schitter (2018) point out that *Prolific* is an extremely valuable tool for online experiments[1] because of its transparency. Potential respondents were aware that they were being recruited for research and had information about expected salaries, rights, and responsibilities. In turn, researchers can preliminarily screen a subject pool in many dimensions. Further, researchers can review the responses received and reject those that they feel are unreliable, for example, because the questionnaire was completed too quickly. Douglas et al. (2023) compared *Prolific* with its competitors, i.e. *MTurk, Qualtrics*, and *Cloud Research*, and found that *Prolific* and *Cloud Research* respondents were characterised by giving valuable answers, remembering previously provided information, having unique IP addresses and geolocations, and working slowly enough to be able to read all questions. *Prolific* also proved to be less expensive than *Cloud Research*.

Sample size and representativeness

The possibility of two potential inference errors is associated with testing the endowment effect hypothesis. The error of the first type concerns the rejection of the null hypothesis, which is not false. To reduce the likelihood of this error, it is necessary to reduce the significance level, which is the a priori acceptable risk for making this error. In this study, a significance level of 10% was adopted, which is common in economics research (Imbens, 2021). By contrast, an error of the second type refers to accepting a null hypothesis that is, in fact, false. To minimise the possibility of a second type of error, the power of the test should be increased by ensuring an adequate test sample size. The literature indicates that a well-designed experiment should have an 80% a priori chance of determining the effect under study. To ensure an analysis power of 80%, the minimum sample size was set at 140 respondents based on the calculated effect size from Gong et al. (2019).[2]

Another aspect of research sample selection is its representativeness. Bao (2020) emphasised that OPDPs are not a good place to conduct research in which the target population is the elderly, as they are underrepresented in these tools. However, most housing transactions in the sales and rental markets are between the ages of 20 and 40, which means that OPDPs can be successfully used to identify the endowment effect (Bao, 2020; Moneta, 2021; Prajsnar, 2023). Ultimately, approximately 400 responses were collected from each of the targeted populations (homeowners and tenants) using quota sampling.[3] Data collection was performed in November 2023.

Questionnaire design

The questionnaire was divided into two parts. The first contains questions characterising the respondent in terms of gender, age, income, education, working situation, place of residence, and attachment to homeownership. These variables were identified as significantly affecting WTA and WTP values based on the previous research presented in Chapter 1 and served as control variables in the model. The second part of the questionnaire included questions about hypothetical housing market situations to elicit WTA and WTP values. The contingent valuation method (CVM) was used as an open-ended question. Following Bao and Gong (2016), Gong et al. (2019), and Bao (2020), sellers (landlords) were asked about the minimum amount they would be willing to accept to sell (rent) a flat and buyers (tenants) were asked about the maximum amount they would be willing to pay for a flat (rent a flat).

Respondents were also given basic information about the hypothetical flat and asked not to consider any financial constraints or transaction costs. The specifics of the hypothetical dwelling have been set to reflect, as far as possible, a typical flat in the local market. Respondents were also informed that it would not be possible to change their answers to questions. This was intended to remove determinants of the WTA-WTP gap other than the endowment effect, that is: (i) information asymmetry (buyers and sellers had the same information regarding the physical characteristics of the hypothetical dwelling and its location); (ii) substitution effect (the specifics of the dwelling have been established to reflect a typical flat); (iii) income effect (respondents were asked not to take budget constraints into account); (iv) transaction costs (respondents were asked not to consider the costs associated with the transaction, e.g. notary fees, taxes); (v) strategic motives (respondents were informed that it would not be possible to change the declared value of WTA and WTP); (vi) transaction demand (respondents were informed that they were interested in doing the transaction but were not compelled to do so.). Respondents were also asked to treat the transacted flat as either an exchange good or a consumer good, depending on the group studied.

The respondents in Panel A (see Table 3.2) were asked to act as sellers of a flat in which they did not live to give the property an exchangeable character. They were first given sales prices of similar properties, followed by information on their changes over the last four years. In the last question, the respondents were asked to provide the value of the WTA after considering their price expectations for the future. Initially, respondents were set on an upward price trend. After the response, the characteristics of the flat changed, and a decreasing trend was set. Next, respondents in this group were asked to provide the value of WTA when they chose to rent the flat instead of selling it. In this case, the WTA value refers to the rent rather than the selling price. Panel B differs from Panel A in its information on the nature of the flat. Specifically, respondents were asked to imagine that they were selling the flat in which they lived so that the object of the transaction had a consumption character for them. Panels C and D deal with simulations of housing buyer behaviour and differ in the nature of the housing good (exchangeable/consumable). Finally, Panels E and F focus on tenants and distinguish the nature of the housing good.

Table 3.2 Questionnaire design.

No.	Exchange/ consumption information	Label	Market trend	Price information
Panel A: Seller-exchange and landlord-exchange				
A1	Seller did not reside in the dwelling	Average market sales price	Up	Similar properties sold between 500,000 and 600,000 PLN
			Down	Similar properties sold between 600,000 and 700,000 PLN
A2		Rate of change of market sales price	Up	Sales prices of similar properties up 20% in 4 years
			Down	Sales prices of similar properties down 20% in 4 years

(Continued)

Table 3.2 (Continued)

No.	Exchange/ consumption information	Label	Market trend	Price information
A3		Sales price expectations	Up Down	Think about the development of sales property prices over the year
A4	Landlord did not reside in the dwelling	Average market rental price	Up	Similar properties rented between 2,000 and 3,000 PLN
			Down	Similar properties rented between 2,500 and 3,500 PLN
A5		Rate of change of market rental price	Up	Rental prices of similar properties up 10% in 4 years
			Down	Rental prices of similar properties down 10% in 4 years
A6		Rental price expectations	Up Down	Think about the development of rental property prices over the year

Panel B: Seller-consumption and landlord-consumption

B1	Seller resided in the dwelling	Average market sales price	Up	Similar properties sold between 500,000 and 600,000 PLN
			Down	Similar properties sold between 600,000 and 700,000 PLN
B2		Rate of change of market sales price	Up	Sales prices of similar properties up 20% in 4 years
			Down	Sales prices of similar properties down 20% in 4 years
B3		Sales price expectations	Up Down	Think about the development of sales property prices over the year
B4	Landlord resided in the dwelling	Average market rental price	Up	Similar properties rented between 2,000 and 3,000 PLN
			Down	Similar properties rented between 2,500 and 3,500 PLN

(*Continued*)

Table 3.2 (Continued)

No.	Exchange/ consumption information	Label	Market trend	Price information
B5		Rate of change of market rental price	Up	Rental prices of similar properties up 10% in 4 years
			Down	Rental prices of similar properties down 10% in 4 years
B6		Rental price expectations	Up	Think about the development of rental property prices over the year
			Down	
Panel C: Buyer-exchange				
C1	Buyer does not want to reside in the dwelling	Average market sales price	Up	Similar properties sold between 500,000 and 600,000 PLN
			Down	Similar properties sold between 600,000 and 700,000 PLN
C2		Rate of change of market sales price	Up	Sales prices of similar properties up 20% in 4 years
			Down	Sales prices of similar properties down 20% in 4 years
C3		Sales price expectations	Up	Think about the development of sales property prices over the year
			Down	
Panel D: Buyer-consumption				
D1	Buyer does want to reside in the dwelling	Average market sales price	Up	Similar properties sold between 500,000 and 600,000 PLN
			Down	Similar properties sold between 600,000 and 700,000 PLN
D2		Rate of change of market sales price	Up	Sales prices of similar properties up 20% in 4 years
			Down	Sales prices of similar properties down 20% in 4 years
D3		Sales price expectations	Up	Think about the development of sales property prices over the year
			Down	

(*Continued*)

Table 3.2 (Continued)

No.	Exchange/ consumption information	Label	Market trend	Price information
Panel E: Tenant-exchange				
E1	Tenant does not want to reside in the dwelling	Average market rental price	Up	Similar properties rented between 2,000 and 3,000 PLN
			Down	Similar properties rented between 2,500 and 3,500 PLN
E2		Rate of change of market rental price	Up	Rental prices of similar properties up 10% in 4 years
			Down	Rental prices of similar properties down 10% in 4 years
E3		Rental price expectations	Up	
			Down	Think about the development of rental property prices over the year
Panel F: Tenant-consumption				
F1	Tenant does want to reside in the dwelling	Average market rental price	Up	Similar properties rented between 2,000 and 3,000 PLN
			Down	Similar properties rented between 2,500 and 3,500 PLN
F2		Rate of change of market rental price	Up	Rental prices of similar properties up 10% in 4 years
			Down	Rental prices of similar properties down 10% in 4 years
F3		Rental price expectations	Up	Think about the development of rental property prices over the year
			Down	

Source: Own study.

Note: For the upward trend, the hypothetical flat was located in the centre of a city with 20,000 people. It was on the 1st floor, and the standard was good. The standard of the building was also good, but the building did not have an elevator. For the decreasing trend, the flat was located in the centre of a city of 200,000 people, with other parameters unchanged. One PLN is equal to 4.4475 Euro on 31.10.2023.

Respondents' characteristics

A total of 407 homeowners and 406 tenants were invited to participate via the *Prolific*. After verifying the responses received, six observations from the first group and nine from the second group were discarded owing to fast or unreliable responses. The number of responses removed represented only 1.85% of the total. The basic descriptive characteristics of the respondents in each panel, as described in the previous section, are shown in Table 3.3. The tenants (panels E and F) are several years younger than homeowners and have lower monthly incomes. Most respondents hold a university degree and are employed. Almost all tenants live in urban areas, in contrast to homeowners, approximately 15% of whom live in the countryside. In addition to Panel F, the predominant belief among respondents was that ownership is the right form of housing tenure. Furthermore, the majority of respondents rated the standard of their current dwelling as at least good, with a higher percentage evident among homeowners. The variation in responses across panels of homeowners and tenants was not large.

3.2.3 *Econometric framework*

To verify the research hypotheses posed in Section 3.2.1, the data collected through a lab-in-the-field experiment will be subjected to econometric modelling. The explanatory variable in the model is the percentage deviation of the reported WTA and WTP values from the benchmark which is the market price/rent, for example $\frac{WTA-benchmark}{benchmark}$. This type of analysis, in relative terms, allows the sales and rental markets to be modelled in a single equation. The model takes the following form.

$$y_i = \beta_0 + \beta_1 upse_i + \beta_2 upsc_i + \beta_3 upbe_i + \beta_4 upbc + \beta_5 downse_i + \beta_6 downsc_i$$
$$+ \beta_7 downbe_i + \beta_8 downbc_i + \alpha_1 uple_i + \alpha_2 uplc_i + \alpha_3 upte_i + \alpha_4 uptc_i$$
$$+ \alpha_5 downle_i + \alpha_6 downlc_i + \alpha_7 downte_i + \delta_1 gen_i + \delta_2 age_i + \delta_3 inc_i$$
$$+ \delta_4 edu_i + \delta_5 emp_i + \delta_6 loc_i + \delta_7 nor_i + \delta_8 std_i + \delta_9 per_i + \varepsilon_i \qquad (4)$$

where: y_i is a percentage deviation of WTA or WTP from the benchmark. The latter is the property market price, which is PLN 550,000 in the up market and PLN 650,000 in the down market for the sales market. In the context of the rental market, the market rent was PLN 2,500 in the up market and PLN 3,000 in the down market; β_0 is the

Table 3.3 Respondents characteristics.

Panel	N	Gender[a]	Age[b]	Income[c]	Education[d]	Employment[e]	Location[f]	Norm[g]	Standard[h]
A	103	W – 39% M – 61%	Less than 20 – 2% Between 20 and 40 – 80% More than 40 – 18%	Less than 4,000 – 25% Between 4,000 and 8,000 – 55% More than 8,000 – 20%	H – 65% O – 35%	E – 79% N – 21%	C – 89% S – 11%	P – 61% NP – 39%	G – 82% O – 18%
B	105	W – 31% M – 69%	Less than 20 – 4% Between 20 and 40 – 72% More than 40 – 24%	Less than 4,000 – 26% Between 4,000 and 8,000 – 49% More than 8,000 – 25%	H – 72% O – 28%	E – 83% N – 17%	C – 88% S – 12%	P – 69% NP – 31%	G – 77% O – 23%
C	100	W – 46% M – 54%	Less than 20 – 1% Between 20 and 40 – 89% More than 40 – 10%	Less than 4,000 – 25% Between 4,000 and 8,000 – 58% More than 8,000 – 17%	H – 67% O – 33%	E – 87% N – 13%	C – 86% S – 14%	P – 74% NP – 26%	G – 87% O – 13%
D	93	W – 41% M – 59%	Less than 20 – 5% Between 20 and 40 – 89% More than 40 – 6%	Less than 4,000 – 35% Between 4,000 and 8,000 – 41% More than 8,000 – 24%	H – 60% O – 40%	E – 73% N – 27%	C – 85% S – 15%	P – 59% NP – 41%	G – 78% O – 22%
E	198	W – 46% M – 54%	Less than 20 – 3% Between 20 and 40 – 95% More than 40 – 2%	Less than 4,000 – 53% Between 4,000 and 8,000 – 39% More than 8,000 – 8%	H – 55% O – 45%	E – 55% N – 45%	C – 99% S – 1%	P – 54% NP – 46%	G – 71% O – 29%
F	199	W – 51% M – 49%	Less than 20 – 6% Between 20 and 40 – 93% More than 40 – 1%	Less than 4,000 – 50% Between 4,000 and 8,000 – 42% More than 8,000 – 8%	H – 50% O – 50%	E – 57% N – 43%	C – 98% S – 2%	P – 47% NP – 53%	G – 63% O – 37%

Source: Own study.

Note: [a] W represents women and M men.
[b] In years.
[c] In PLN.
[d] H represents higher education and O other.
[e] E represents employed and N is not employed.
[f] C represents city and S countryside.
[g] P represents that social norm is present and NP is not present.
[h] G represents at least good standard and O other.

model constant; $\beta_1,...,\beta_8$ and $\alpha_1,...,\alpha_7$ and $\delta_1,...,\delta_9$ are the parameters of the model; ε_i is the error term; $upse_i$ ($downse_i$) takes the value 1 if the respondent has acted as a seller of the dwelling as an exchange good during up (down) market or 0 otherwise; $upsc_i$ ($downsc_i$) takes the value 1 if the respondent has acted as a seller of the dwelling as a consumer good during up (down) market or 0 otherwise; $upbe_i$ ($downbe_i$) takes the value 1 if the respondent has acted as a buyer of the dwelling as an exchange good during up (down) market or 0 otherwise; $upbc_i$ ($downbc_i$) takes the value 1 if the respondent has acted as a buyer of the dwelling as a consumer good during up (down) market or 0 otherwise; $uple_i$ ($downle_i$) takes the value 1 if the respondent has acted as a landlord of the dwelling as an exchange good during up (down) market or 0 otherwise; $uplc_i$ ($downlc_i$) takes the value 1 if the respondent has acted as a landlord of the dwelling as a consumer good during up (down) market or 0 otherwise; $upte_i$ ($downte_i$) takes the value 1 if the respondent has acted as a tenant of the dwelling as an exchange good during up (down) market or 0 otherwise; $uptc_i$ takes the value 1 if the respondent has acted as a tenant of the dwelling as a consumer good during up market or 0 otherwise; gen_i takes the value 1 if female or 0 if male; age_i is the respondent's age; inc_i is the respondent's gross monthly income; edu_i takes the value 1 if the respondent has a higher education or 0 otherwise; emp_i takes the value 1 if the respondent is employed and 0 otherwise; loc_i takes the value of 1 if the respondent lives in a urban area and 0 otherwise; nor_i takes the value of 1 if the respondent agrees with the social norm that ownership is the right form of housing tenure; std_i takes the value of 1 if the respondent assesses the condition of their dwelling to be at least good; per_i denotes the percentage change in property prices given to respondents during the experiment.

In this model, the constant β_0 represents the mean deviation of WTP values reported by tenants who treated the transacted dwelling as a consumer good during the down market with other variables held fixed. This group was considered as a baseline because for it the mean value of the dependent variable is the lowest among all the groups studied, which will allow a simple interpretation of the regression coefficients obtained. The parameters $\beta_1,...,\beta_8$ and $\alpha_1,...,\alpha_7$ report by how much the dependent variable decreases/increases on average for other respondent groups. In this framework, estimating the percentage WTA-WTP gap involves calculating the difference between the selected parameters of Equation (4). For example, the expression $\beta_1-\beta_3$ denotes the size of the endowment effect as a percentage of the property market price in the sales housing market during the up market when both seller and buyer treat the housing good as an exchange good. In order to calculate the endowment effect in absolute terms, i.e. as an amount, the expression $\beta_1 - \beta_3$ should be multiplied by the adopted benchmark. Using Equation 4, the research hypotheses can be tested, as shown in Table 3.4.

Table 3.4 Econometric procedure for hypotheses H1–H6.

Hypothesis H1			
Sales housing market		Seller-exchange	Seller-consumption
Buyer-exchange	Up market	$\beta_1 > \beta_3$	$\beta_2 > \beta_3$
	Down market	$\beta_5 > \beta_7$	$\beta_6 > \beta_7$
Buyer-	Up market	$\beta_1 > \beta_4$	$\beta_2 > \beta_4$
consumption	Down market	$\beta_5 > \beta_8$	$\beta_6 > \beta_8$

Hypothesis H2			
Rental housing market		Landlord-exchange	Landlord-consumption
Tenant-	Up market	$\alpha_1 > \alpha_3$	$\alpha_2 > \alpha_3$
exchange	Down market	$\alpha_5 > \alpha_7$	$\alpha_6 > \alpha_7$
Tenant-	Up market	$\alpha_1 > \alpha_4$	$\alpha_2 > \alpha_4$
consumption	Down market	$\alpha_5 > 0$	$\alpha_6 > 0$

Hypothesis H3

Sales housing market
$$\frac{\beta_1-\beta_3+\beta_2-\beta_3+\beta_1-\beta_4+\beta_2-\beta_4}{4} > \frac{\beta_5-\beta_7+\beta_6-\beta_7+\beta_5-\beta_8+\beta_6-\beta_8}{4}$$

Rental housing market
$$\frac{\alpha_1-\alpha_3+\alpha_2-\alpha_3+\alpha_1-\alpha_4+\alpha_2-\alpha_4}{4} > \frac{\alpha_5-\alpha_7+\alpha_6-\alpha_7+\alpha_5+\alpha_6}{4}$$

Hypothesis H4

Sales housing market
$$\frac{\beta_1-\beta_3+\beta_5-\beta_7+\beta_1-\beta_4+\beta_5-\beta_8}{4} < \frac{\beta_2-\beta_3+\beta_6-\beta_7+\beta_2-\beta_4+\beta_6-\beta_8}{4}$$

Hypothesis H5

Rental housing market
$$\frac{\alpha_1-\alpha_3+\alpha_5-\alpha_7+\alpha_1-\alpha_4+\alpha_5}{4} < \frac{\alpha_2-\alpha_3+\alpha_6-\alpha_7+\alpha_2-\alpha_4+\alpha_6}{4}$$

Hypothesis H6

Sales housing market vs. rental housing market
$$\frac{\beta_1-\beta_3+\beta_2-\beta_3+\beta_5-\beta_7+\beta_6-\beta_7+\beta_1-\beta_4+\beta_2-\beta_4+\beta_5-\beta_8+\beta_6-\beta_8}{8}$$
$$> \frac{\alpha_1-\alpha_3+\alpha_2-\alpha_3+\alpha_5-\alpha_7+\alpha_6-\alpha_7+\alpha_1-\alpha_4+\alpha_2-\alpha_4+\alpha_5+\alpha_6}{8}$$

Source: Own study.

Note: When the seller/landlord of a dwelling treats it as an exchange good, the entire primary market and a part of the secondary market are examined. When the seller/landlord of a dwelling treats it as a consumer good, a part of the secondary market is investigated. If the endowment effect is greater when the seller/landlord of a dwelling treats it as a consumer good, the endowment effect will always be greater in the secondary market than in the primary market, as these types of transactions occur only in the former.

3.2.4   Results and discussion

Table 3.5 shows the mean WTA and WTP values and the mean per-centage deviation of these values from the adopted benchmarks. Having received all the information on the development of the property market during its upward trend, respondents acting as sellers or landlords tend to set the WTA value above the market price of the dwelling. The largest deviation of +6.43%, on average, occurs for sellers of a dwelling as a consumer good. Similarly, buyers and tenants tend to set WTP values below the accepted benchmarks. In this case, the most extreme WTP values are reported on average (−7.70%) by buyers of the dwelling as a consumer good. In contrast, during the down market, the supply side of the market generally set WTA values on par with the market value of the property, with the exception of landlords treating the dwelling as an exchange good whose average WTA value was below the accepted benchmark. In contrast, the demand side of the market, that is, buyers and tenants, is characterised by significantly lower WTP values than the market price of the dwelling (on average between −11.58% and −14.92%). The results obtained are partly in line with Weaver and Frederick's (2012) reference price theory and the theoretical considerations presented in Chapter 2. Unexpectedly, buyers/tenants are willing to pay, on average, an amount significantly less than the market value of the dwelling, whereas theory predicts that the WTP value should be equal to the assumed benchmark. This situation increases the strength of the endowment effect due to the widening of the WTA-WTP gap.

Table 3.6 shows the preliminary estimates of the WTA-WTP gap for the different segments of the housing market. Based on these estimates, it can be concluded that the endowment effect is present in the sales and rental housing markets, regardless of whether the transacted dwelling is treated as an exchange or consumer good. The latter implies that the effect under study is found in both the primary and secondary markets. However, based on Table 3.6, it is not possible to clearly assess whether the endowment effect is stronger in times of price increases in the housing market or in times of price decreases. Furthermore, it is evident that the endowment effect is stronger in secondary markets, that is, where there are transactions in which the seller or landlord treats the housing good as a consumption good. Finally, it can also be seen that the WTA-WTP gaps are generally larger in the sales market than in the rental housing market. However, the estimates

Table 3.5 Respondents' WTA or WTP values.

Panel	Mean absolute values						Mean percentage deviation from the benchmark*	
	WTA or WTP PI: Actual market sales/rental prices		WTA or WTP PI: Rate of change of sales/rental prices		WTA or WTP PI: Sales/Rental price expectations		WTA or WTP PI: Sales/Rental price expectations	
	Up market	Down market	Up market	Down market	Up market	Down market	Up market	Down market
A-S†	513,757	642,476	571,175	630,116	567,437 (p ≤ 0.05)	637,816 (p > 0.05)	3.17%	−1.87%
A-L‡	2,387	2,886	2,548	2,779	2,580 (p ≤ 0.05)	2,787 (p ≤ 0.01)	3.22%	−7.09%
B-S†	520,952	653,619	585,276	644,190	585,381 (p ≤ 0.01)	654,429 (p > 0.05)	6.43%	0.68%
B-L‡	2,415	2,941	2,599	2,880	2,628 (p ≤ 0.01)	2,903 (p > 0.05)	5.12%	−3.22%
C	468,150	597,467	517,750	564,117	522,700 (p ≤ 0.05)	574,717 (p ≤ 0.01)	−4.96%	−11.58%
D	463,161	589,677	499,989	552,742	507,634 (p ≤ 0.01)	558,204 (p ≤ 0.01)	−7.70%	−14.12%
E	2,137	2,637	2,343	2,538	2,385 (p ≤ 0.01)	2,558 (p ≤ 0.01)	−4.61%	−14.72%
F	2,152	2,655	2,381	2,542	2,381 (p ≤ 0.01)	2,553 (p ≤ 0.01)	−4.76%	−14.92%

Source: Own study.

Note: Values shown are in the PLN. One PLN is equal to 4.4475 Euro on 31.10.2023.

† This applies to the seller.

‡ This applies to the landlord.

* The benchmark was the property market price, which for the sales market was PLN 550,000 in the up market and PLN 650,000 in the down market. In the context of the rental market, the market rental price was PLN 2,500 in up market and PLN 3,000 in the down market. P-values represent the results of a one-sample *t*-test between the average WTA or WTP and the property market price. PI means price information.

Table 3.6 Preliminary estimates of the WTA-WTP gap.

Sales housing market		Seller-exchange	Seller-consumption
Buyer-exchange	Up market	3.17%+4.96% =8.13%	6.43%+4.96% =11.39%
	Down market	−1.87%+11.58% =9.71%	0.68%+11.58% =12.26%
Buyer-consumption	Up market	3.17%+7.70% =10.87%	6.43%+7.70% =14.13%
	Down market	−1.87%+14.12% =12.25%	0.68%+14.12% =14.80%
Rental housing market		Landlord-exchange	Landlord-consumption
Tenant-exchange	Up market	3.22%+4.61% =7.83%	5.12%+4.61% =9.73%
	Down market	−7.09%+14.72% =7.63%	−3.22%+14.72% =11.50%
Tenant-consumption	Up market	3.22%+4.76% =7.98%	5.12%+4.76% =9.88%
	Down market	−7.09%+14.92% =7.83%	−3.22%+14.92% =11.70%

Source: Own study.

in Table 3.6 do not take into account other potential variables affecting the value of WTA and WTP, and the comparisons of WTA-WTP gaps are not based on formal statistical tests, which do not allow at this stage of the study to verify the research hypotheses.

Table 3.7 shows the results of the estimation of the model presented in Equation (4). The predictor *per* has been removed due to collinearity. For the remaining independent variables, the variance inflation factor (VIF) value did not exceed two, indicating that the correlation between them was low. The R^2 coefficient is equal to 0.1376 which is similar to previous studies on the endowment effect in the housing market done by Bao and Gong (2016) and Gong et al. (2019). The model uses the sandwich estimator of variance to account for heteroscedasticity. Furthermore, the link and Ramsey RESET tests indicated that the model was correctly specified.

The obtained model parameters indicate that among the control variables, only three significantly affect the dependent variable. First, an increase in the respondent's income contributes to the possibility of overestimating the respondent's reported WTA or WTP relative to

Table 3.7 Model parameters – equation 4.

Variable	Coefficient	Robust standard error[†]	t-statistic	P-value	Variance inflation factor
Constant	−0.1926*	0.0251	−7.69	0.0000	–
upse	0.1640*	0.0191	8.59	0.0000	1.50
upsc	0.1974*	0.0253	7.79	0.0000	1.55
upbe	0.0790*	0.0244	3.24	0.0010	1.50
upbc	0.0576	0.0276	2.09	0.0370	1.43
downse	0.1135*	0.0182	6.23	0.0000	1.50
downsc	0.1399*	0.0203	6.89	0.0000	1.55
downbe	0.0128	0.0217	0.59	0.5560	1.50
downbc	−0.0066	0.0234	−0.28	0.7790	1.43
uple	0.1645*	0.0202	8.14	0.0000	1.50
uplc	0.1843*	0.0231	7.99	0.0000	1.55
upte	0.1021*	0.0199	5.13	0.0000	1.81
uptc	0.1015*	0.0201	5.04	0.0000	1.80
downle	0.0614*	0.0188	3.26	0.0010	1.50
downlc	0.1009*	0.0218	4.63	0.0000	1.55
downte	0.0010	0.0172	0.06	0.9560	1.81
gen	−0.0044	0.0087	−0.50	0.6140	1.11
age	−0.0006	0.0005	−1.08	0.2820	1.48
inc	0.000004*	0.0000	3.02	0.0030	1.44
edu	−0.0058	0.0101	−0.58	0.5610	1.34
emp	0.0304*	0.0121	2.51	0.0120	1.56
loc	0.0030	0.0155	0.19	0.8460	1.06
nor	−0.0013	0.0087	−0.15	0.8800	1.04
std	0.0406*	0.0098	4.13	0.0000	1.07
per	Omitted due to collinearity				
R^2	0.1376				
N	2,012				
Link test for model specification[‡]	$p=0.54$				
Ramsey RESET test for model specification[‡]	$p=0.43$				

Source: Own study.

Note: [†] Heteroskedasticity-consistent standard errors.

[‡] H_0: Model is correctly specified.

* Significant at least at the 0.10 level. The normality of the residuals of the model was not tested due to the large sample size, which makes it possible to conclude that the OLS (ordinary least squares) estimator is approximately normally distributed (Wooldridge, 2018).

the market sales/rental price of the dwelling, thus confirming the results obtained by Bao and Gong (2016). As noted by the latter authors,
the elevated WTA or WTP estimates made by respondents with higher
incomes may be due to income constraints that are deeply rooted in
the minds of respondents. Therefore, they were unconsciously guided
by their financial situation when participating in the experiment. The
second significant control variable was employment, which was positively related to the dependent variable. This relationship is in line with
Bao and Gong's (2016) study. In this case, respondents, especially those
acting as buyers and tenants, may have been more likely to report elevated WTP values because of their higher purchasing power in real life.
Again, the impact of being employed may have been unconscious, as
respondents participated in a fictitious experiment and were instructed
that the hypothetical transaction would not affect their financial situation. The last control variable that significantly affected the dependent
variable was the standard of dwelling in which the respondent actually
lived. Again, the relationship is positive and indicates that respondents
living in housing of at least a good standard tend to report WTA or WTP
values above the market value. However, it seems that, in this case, this
situation will mainly apply to respondents acting as sellers or landlords.
The latter may also be unconsciously influenced by their property, as a
better standard automatically implies a higher value.

When analysing the significance of the parameters for the different
groups of respondents, it should be noted that only for three of them,
the estimated parameter turned out to be non-significantly different
from zero. This applies to respondents who act as buyers or tenants in
the down market. Given that the constant in the model is for tenants
acting during the down market and treating the dwelling as a consumer
good, this result is as expected, since, as can be seen in Table 3.5, the
mean deviations of WTP values between buyers and tenants during the
down market are very similar.

Table 3.8 shows the size of the WTA-WTP gaps based on the model
estimates and thus the intensity of the endowment effect in the residential sales and rental market, distinguishing between primary and
secondary markets. In general, the estimated WTA-WTP gaps are
of a similar magnitude to those presented in Table 3.6. The average
magnitude of the endowment effect in the sales market was 11.95% in
relative terms, and PLN 72,086 in absolute terms. By contrast, in the
rental market, the endowment effect was 7.69%, or PLN 212. Table 3.8
shows that the average strength of the endowment effect is greater

Table 3.8 Estimates of the WTA-WTP gap based on the model.

Sales housing market		Seller-exchange	Seller-consumption
Buyer-exchange	Up market	8.50%	11.84%
	Down market	11.35%	13.99%
Buyer-	Up market	10.63%	13.98%
consumption	Down market	11.35%	13.99%
Mean		10.46% (PLN 63,199)	13.45% (PLN 80,973)
Overall mean		11.95% (PLN 72,086)	
Rental housing market		Landlord-exchange	Landlord-consumption
Tenant-exchange	Up market	6.24%	8.22%
	Down market	6.14%	10.09%
Tenant-	Up market	6.29%	8.28%
consumption	Down market	6.14%	10.09%
Mean		6.20% (PLN 170)	9.17% (PLN 254)
Overall mean		7.69% (PLN 212)	

Source: Own study.

Note: 1 PLN is equal to 4.4475 Euro on 31.10.2023. Calculations were performed assuming a coefficient value equal to 0, if the model estimates indicated that it was not statistically significant.

when the supply side treats the object of the transaction as a consumer good – in the sales market by 2.99 percentage points and in the rental market by 2.97 percentage points. Simultaneously, this situation implies that the endowment effect is stronger in secondary markets than in primary markets, as only in the former are transactions in which sellers or landlords have previously used transacted dwellings. It can also be seen from Table 3.8 that there is a difference of 4.26 percentage points between the average intensity of the endowment effect between the sales and rental housing markets, in favour of the former. Looking at the WTA-WTP gap estimates, it is not clear whether the endowment effect varies according to the housing market cycle phase. In general, endowment effects across the up and down markets are very similar.

Table 3.9 shows the statistical verification of the research hypotheses. The procedure was started each time by performing a two-sided heteroskedasticity-robust F test using an F statistic and an F distribution to calculate the significance level of the hypothesis test. If the estimated p-value indicated rejection of the null hypothesis, one proceeded to the appropriate one-sided test, as indicated in Table 3.4.

Table 3.9 Verification of research hypotheses.

Hypothesis H1

Sales housing market		Seller-exchange	Seller-consumption
Buyer-exchange	Up market	$\beta_1 = \beta_3 \ (p < 0.01)$	$\beta_2 = \beta_3 \ (p < 0.01)$
		$\beta_1 > \beta_3 \ (p > 0.99)$	$\beta_2 > \beta_3 \ (p > 0.99)$
	Down market	$\beta_5 = \beta_7 \ (p < 0.01)$	$\beta_6 = \beta_7 \ (p < 0.01)$
		$\beta_5 > \beta_7 \ (p > 0.99)$	$\beta_6 > \beta_7 \ (p > 0.99)$
Buyer-consumption	Up market	$\beta_1 = \beta_4 \ (p < 0.01)$	$\beta_2 = \beta_4 \ (p < 0.01)$
		$\beta_1 > \beta_4 \ (p > 0.99)$	$\beta_2 > \beta_4 \ (p > 0.99)$
	Down market	$\beta_5 = \beta_8 \ (p < 0.01)$	$\beta_6 = \beta_8 \ (p < 0.01)$
		$\beta_5 > \beta_8 \ (p > 0.99)$	$\beta_6 > \beta_8 \ (p > 0.99)$

Hypothesis H2

Rental housing market		Landlord-exchange	Landlord-consumption
Tenant-exchange	Up market	$\alpha_1 = \alpha_3 \ (p < 0.01)$	$\alpha_2 = \alpha_3 \ (p < 0.01)$
		$\alpha_1 > \alpha_3 \ (p > 0.99)$	$\alpha_2 > \alpha_3 \ (p > 0.99)$
	Down market	$\alpha_5 = \alpha_7 \ (p < 0.01)$	$\alpha_6 = \alpha_7 \ (p < 0.01)$
		$\alpha_5 > \alpha_7 \ (p > 0.99)$	$\alpha_6 > \alpha_7 \ (p > 0.99)$
Tenant-consumption	Up market	$\alpha_1 = \alpha_4 \ (p < 0.01)$	$\alpha_2 = \alpha_4 \ (p < 0.01)$
		$\alpha_1 > \alpha_4 \ (p > 0.99)$	$\alpha_2 > \alpha_4 \ (p > 0.99)$
	Down market	$\alpha_5 = 0 \ (p < 0.01)$	$\alpha_6 = 0 \ (p < 0.01)$
		$\alpha_5 > 0 \ (p > 0.99)$	$\alpha_6 > 0 \ (p > 0.99)$

Hypothesis H3

Sales housing market

$$\frac{\beta_1-\beta_3+\beta_2-\beta_3+\beta_1-\beta_4+\beta_2-\beta_4}{4} = \frac{\beta_5-\beta_7+\beta_6-\beta_7+\beta_5-\beta_8+\beta_6-\beta_8}{4}$$

$(p=0.69)$

Rental housing market

$$\frac{\alpha_1-\alpha_3+\alpha_2-\alpha_3+\alpha_1-\alpha_4+\alpha_2-\alpha_4}{4} = \frac{\alpha_5-\alpha_7+\alpha_6-\alpha_7+\alpha_5+\alpha_6}{4}$$

$(p=0.71)$

Hypothesis H4

Sales housing market

$$\frac{\beta_1-\beta_3+\beta_5-\beta_7+\beta_1-\beta_4+\beta_5-\beta_8}{4} = \frac{\beta_2-\beta_3+\beta_6-\beta_7+\beta_2-\beta_4+\beta_6-\beta_8}{4}$$

$(p=0.07)$

$$\frac{\beta_1-\beta_3+\beta_5-\beta_7+\beta_1-\beta_4+\beta_5-\beta_8}{4} < \frac{\beta_2-\beta_3+\beta_6-\beta_7+\beta_2-\beta_4+\beta_6-\beta_8}{4}$$

$(p=0.79)$

Hypothesis H5

Rental housing market

$$\frac{\alpha_1-\alpha_3+\alpha_5-\alpha_7+\alpha_1-\alpha_4+\alpha_5}{4} = \frac{\alpha_2-\alpha_3+\alpha_6-\alpha_7+\alpha_2-\alpha_4+\alpha_6}{4}$$

$(p=0.08)$

$$\frac{\alpha_1-\alpha_3+\alpha_5-\alpha_7+\alpha_1-\alpha_4+\alpha_5}{4} < \frac{\alpha_2-\alpha_3+\alpha_6-\alpha_7+\alpha_2-\alpha_4+\alpha_6}{4}$$

$(p=0.96)$

(*Continued*)

Table 3.9 (Continued)

Hypothesis H6

Sales housing
market
vs. rental
housing
market

$$\frac{\beta_1-\beta_3+\beta_2-\beta_3+\beta_5-\beta_7+\beta_6-\beta_7+\beta_1-\beta_4+\beta_2-\beta_4+\beta_5-\beta_8+\beta_6-\beta_8}{8}$$

$$=\frac{\alpha_1-\alpha_3+\alpha_2-\alpha_3+\alpha_5-\alpha_7+\alpha_6-\alpha_7+\alpha_1-\alpha_4+\alpha_2-\alpha_4+\alpha_5+\alpha_6}{8}$$

$(p=0.02)$

$$\frac{\beta_1-\beta_3+\beta_2-\beta_3+\beta_5-\beta_7+\beta_6-\beta_7+\beta_1-\beta_4+\beta_2-\beta_4+\beta_5-\beta_8+\beta_6-\beta_8}{8}$$

$$>\frac{\alpha_1-\alpha_3+\alpha_2-\alpha_3+\alpha_5-\alpha_7+\alpha_6-\alpha_7+\alpha_1-\alpha_4+\alpha_2-\alpha_4+\alpha_5+\alpha_6}{8}$$

$(p=0.99)$

Source: Own study.

Note: F test was used to test the hypotheses. Hypothesis verification is also intact when p-values are adjusted using the Benjamini and Hochberg (1995) procedure to take into account the multiple testing problem.

The results obtained fully confirmed the earlier estimates presented in Tables 3.6 and 3.8. In particular, in all cases analysed, the estimated coefficients for sellers or landlords are significantly larger than the corresponding coefficients for buyers or tenants. This indicates the presence of a statistically significant endowment effect in the primary and secondary residential sales and rental markets. **Hypotheses H1 and H2 are therefore confirmed**.

On average, the strength of the endowment effect during the up market was not found to be significantly different from its intensity during the down market, implying **the rejection of hypothesis H3**. The latter hypothesis is based on the assumption that price corrections would be higher among sellers and landlords than among buyers and tenants. However, as it turned out, the demand side of the market is not willing to set WTP values close to the market price/rent of the property, as predicted by the reference price theory. The results obtained in this respect are consistent with the lack of consensus on the impact of the property market cycle on the strength of the endowment effect. As indicated in Chapter 1, empirical results in the work of Bao and Gong (2016), for example, indicate an increased intensity of the endowment effect during the up market, while Bao's (2020) estimates show that the endowment effect only occurs during the down market. Finally, Gong et al. (2019) did not find a significant effect of the housing market cycle on the strength of the endowment effect.

Statistical verification also indicated that when the subject of transactions is dwellings treated by sellers or landlords as consumer goods,
on average, the endowment effect is statistically stronger than when
these groups treat dwellings sold/rented as exchangeable goods. As indicated earlier, this situation directly implies that the endowment effect
is stronger in secondary markets than in primary markets, making it
possible to **confirm hypotheses H4 and H5**. In general, these findings are in line with the standard literature on the endowment effect
described in Chapter 1, according to which the endowment effect is
weaker when exchanged goods are transacted. In the context of the
housing literature, the results obtained are in line with the study by
Cheung et al. (2023). Finally, the mean endowment effect was found to
be statistically stronger in the sales market than in the rental housing
market, **confirming hypothesis H6**.

3.3   Summary

Based on the empirical research conducted, it is possible to answer the
research question posed in Chapter 3.

*RQ6. Is there an endowment effect on the Polish housing market? If
so, does the magnitude of the endowment effect differ between sales
and rental markets, and across primary and secondary markets?*

The empirical research and the subsequent verification of the research
hypotheses clearly indicate that the endowment effect significantly
shapes the Polish residential market. On the sales housing market it
amounts on average to 11.95%, i.e. PLN 72,086, while in the rental
market, it amounts on average to 7.69%, that is, PLN 212. This difference in the strength of the endowment effect between the sales and
rental markets proved to be statistically significant in favour of the
former. The endowment effect is also significantly smaller, on average, in primary markets, where sellers/landlords treat the dwellings
they sell/rent as exchange goods. In this case, its magnitude averaged
10.46% (PLN 63,199) in the sales market and 6.20% (PLN 170) in the
rental market. When the supply side treated the object of the transaction as a consumer good, the endowment effect averaged 13.45% (PLN
80,973) in the sales market and 9.17% (PLN 254) in the rental market.
However, the study did not confirm the hypothesis that the endowment
effect varies depending on the housing market cycle phase.

Notes

1 Gangadharan et al. (2022) indicate that an online experiment is a form of lab-in-the-field experiment.
2 The effect size was calculated based on the correlation coefficient estimated as the square of the coefficient of determination reported in Table 1 for Model 1 in the study by Gong et al. (2019). For more on sample size, in the context of the power of analysis, see the review by Serdar et al. (2021).
3 Quota selection is commonly used in behavioural studies (for example, Levy et al. (2020); Bao (2020); Bao and Saunders (2023)). The number of respondents was selected based on the results of comparable studies. For example, Bao (2020) used data from 319 respondents (155 sellers and 164 buyers) when identifying the endowment effect. Gong et al. (2019) had 111 data records from homeowners and 237 from homebuyers.

References

Asal, M. (2019). Is there a bubble in the Swedish housing market? *Journal of European Real Estate Research, 12*(1), 32–61. https://doi.org/10.1108/JERER-03-2018-0013

Bao, H. X. (2020). *Behavioural science and housing decision making.* Routledge.

Bao, H. X., & Gong, C. M. (2016). Endowment effect and housing decisions. *International Journal of Strategic Property Management, 20*(4), 341–353. https://doi.org/10.3846/1648715X.2016.1192069

Bao, H. X., & Saunders, R. (2023). Reference dependence in the UK housing market. *Housing Studies, 38*(7), 1191–1219. https://doi.org/10.1080/02673037.2021.1935767

Benjamini, Y., & Hochberg, Y. (1995). Controlling the false discovery rate: A practical and powerful approach to multiple testing. *Journal of the Royal Statistical Society: Series B (Methodological), 57*(1), 289–300. https://doi.org/10.1111/j.2517-6161.1995.tb02031.x

Bourassa, S. C., Hoesli, M., & Oikarinen, E. (2019). Measuring house price bubbles. *Real Estate Economics, 47*(2), 534–563. https://doi.org/10.1111/1540-6229.12154

Brzezicka, J. (2014). Zjawisko kaskady informacyjnej na rynku nieruchomości. *Ekonomia. Rynek, Gospodarka, Społeczeństwo, 39*, 7–27.

Brzezicka, J. (2016). Znaczenie heurystyki zakotwiczenia i dostosowania w procesie wartościotwórczym na rynku nieruchomości. *Acta Scientiarum Polonorum Administratio Locorum, 15*(1), 31–44.

Brzezicka, J., Radzewicz, A., Kuryj-Wysocka, O., & Wiśniewski, R. (2013). Badanie efektu pewności i izolacji na rynku nieruchomości w kontekście teorii perspektywy. *Studia ekonomiczne, 4*, 560–582.

Brzezicka, J., & Tomal, M. (2023). Estimation of the utility function of money and housing based on the cumulative prospect theory. *Real Estate Management and Valuation, 31*(3), 83–92. https://doi.org/10.2478/remav-2023-0024

Brzezicka, J., & Wiśniewski, R. (2013). Ekonomia behawioralna a rynek nieruchomości–teoria i praktyka. *Psychologia Ekonomiczna, 3*, 6–19.

Brzezicka, J., Wisniewski, R., & Figurska, M. (2018). Disequilibrium in the real estate market: Evidence from Poland. *Land Use Policy, 78*, 515–531. https://doi.org/10.1016/j.landusepol.2018.06.013

Brzezicka, J., Wiśniewski, R., & Walacik, M. (2015). Behawioralne aspekty percepcji wartości na rynku nieruchomości. *Kwartalnik Naukowy Uczelni Vistula, 1*(43), 66–81.

Cheung, K. S., Wong, S. K., & Chung, Y. Y. (2023). Endowment effects of shared ownership: Evidence from Hong Kong. *Housing, Theory and Society.* https://doi.org/10.1080/14036096.2023.2265356

Douglas, B. D., Ewell, P. J., & Brauer, M. (2023). Data quality in online human-subjects research: Comparisons between MTurk, Prolific, CloudResearch, Qualtrics, and SONA. *PLoS ONE, 18*(3), e0279720. https://doi.org/10.1371/journal.pone.0279720

Gangadharan, L., Jain, T., Maitra, P., & Vecci, J. (2022). Lab-in-the-field experiments: Perspectives from research on gender. *The Japanese Economic Review, 73*(1), 31–59. https://doi.org/10.1007/s42973-021-00088-6

Gong, C. M., Lizieri, C., & Bao, H. X. (2019). "Smarter information, smarter consumers"? Insights into the housing market. *Journal of Business Research, 97*, 51–64. https://doi.org/10.1016/j.jbusres.2018.12.036

Hegedüs, J., Lux, M., & Horváth, V. (2018). *Private rental housing in transition countries. An alternative to owner.* Palgrave Macmillan.

Imbens, G. W. (2021). Statistical significance, p-values, and the reporting of uncertainty. *Journal of Economic Perspectives, 35*(3), 157–174. https://doi.org/10.1257/jep.35.3.157

Kahneman, D., & Tversky, A. (1979). Prospect theory: An analysis of decision under risk. *Econometrica, 47*(2), 263–292. https://doi.org/10.2307/1914185

Kokot, S. (2023). The effect of price anchoring on the housing market based on studies of local markets in Poland. *Real Estate Management and Valuation, 31*(3), 44–57. https://doi.org/10.2478/remav-2023-0020

Levy, D. S., Frethey-Bentham, C., & Cheung, W. K. S. (2020). Asymmetric framing effects and market familiarity: Experimental evidence from the real estate market. *Journal of Property Research, 37*(1), 85–104. https://doi.org/10.1080/09599916.2020.1713858

Lux, M., & Sunega, P. (2014). Public housing in the post-socialist states of Central and Eastern Europe: Decline and an open future. *Housing Studies, 29*(4), 501–519. https://doi.org/10.1080/0267303 7.2013.875986

Lux, M., & Sunega, P. (2020). Using path dependence theory to explain housing regime change: The traps of super-homeownership. *Critical Housing Analysis, 7*(1), 25–35. https://doi.org/10.13060/2 3362839.2020.7.1.501

Moneta, M. (2021). *Mieszkanie a wiek kupującego. Sprawdzamy, jakie wymagania i możliwości mają nabywcy w kolejnych dekadach życia.* Bankier. Retrieved February 29, 2024, from www.bankier. pl/wiadomosc/Mieszkanie-a-wiek-kupujacego-Sprawdzamy-jakie-wymagania-i-mozliwosci-maja-nabywcy-w-kolejnych-dekadach-zycia-8244582.html

Palan, S., & Schitter, C. (2018). Prolific.ac – A subject pool for online experiments. *Journal of Behavioral and Experimental Finance, 17*, 22–27. https://doi.org/10.1016/j.jbef.2017.12.004

Prajsnar, A. (2023). *W jakim wieku Polacy kupują mieszkania? Są nowe i ciekawe dane.* Forsal. Retrieved February 29, 2024, from https://forsal.pl/nieruchomosci/mieszkania/artykuly/8724604,w-jakim-wieku-polacy-kupuja-mieszkania-sa-nowe-i-ciekawe-dane.html

Rubaszek, M., & Czerniak, A. (2017). Preferencje Polaków dotyczące struktury własnościowej mieszkań: opis wyników ankiety. *Bank i Kredyt, 48*(2), 197–234.

Serdar, C. C., Cihan, M., Yücel, D., & Serdar, M. A. (2021). Sample size, power and effect size revisited: Simplified and practical approaches in pre-clinical, clinical and laboratory studies. *Biochemia Medica, 31*(1), 27–53. https://doi.org/10.11613/BM.2021.010502

Tomal, M. (2022a). Identification of house price bubbles using robust methodology: Evidence from Polish provincial capitals. *Journal of Housing and the Built Environment, 37*(3), 1461–1488. https://doi. org/10.1007/s10901-021-09903-3

Tomal, M. (2022b). Drivers behind the accuracy of self-reported home valuations: Evidence from an emerging economy. *Journal of European Real Estate Research, 15*(3), 425–443. https://doi.org/10.1108/ JERER-02-2022-0004

Tomal, M. (2023a). The applicability of self-reported home values in housing wealth inequality assessment: Evidence from an emerging country. *Housing Studies*. https://doi.org/10.1080/02673037.2022. 2123902

Tomal, M. (2023b). The COVID-19 pandemic and house price convergence in Poland. *Journal of Housing and the Built Environment*. https://doi.org/10.1007/s10901-023-10090-6

Trojanek, R., Gluszak, M., Tanas, J., & van de Minne, A. (2023). Detecting housing bubble in Poland: Investigation into two housing booms. *Habitat International*, *140*, 102928. https://doi.org/10. 1016/j.habitatint.2023.102928

Tversky, A., & Kahneman, D. (1974). Judgment under uncertainty: Heuristics and biases: Biases in judgments reveal some heuristics of thinking under uncertainty. *Science*, *185*(4157), 1124–1131. https:// doi.org/10.1126/science.185.4157.1124

Weaver, R., & Frederick, S. (2012). A reference price theory of the endowment effect. *Journal of Marketing Research*, *49*(5), 696–707. https://doi.org/10.1509/jmr.09.0103

Wooldridge, J. M. (2018). *Introductory econometrics: A modern approach*. Cengage.

Conclusions

Main findings

This monograph aimed to (i) provide an overview of research on the endowment effect in the housing market, (ii) develop a theoretical model explaining the magnitude of endowment effects in sales and rental housing markets with a distinction between primary and secondary markets, and (iii) assess the presence of endowment effects in the sales and rental housing markets in Poland. All the stated objectives were met. The endowment effect has so far been a little-researched phenomenon in the housing market, but the results of the studies to date have been consistent, that is, this behavioural bias significantly shapes the decision-making of housing market participants. The literature review revealed problems related to the measurement of the endowment effect in the housing market as well as research gaps in this area, which included the lack of a unified theory of multiple reference points in the context of the endowment effect, as well as a lack of work analysing the intensity of this effect in different segments of the housing market. Chapter 2 attempted to fill some of the identified research gaps. A theoretical model of the strength of the endowment effect, based on multiple reference points for different housing market segments, was developed. The model analyses residential sales and rental markets in the primary and secondary markets. In Chapter 3, empirical research was conducted to test the theoretical assumptions conceptualised in Chapter 2. The results of this research revealed that the endowment effect is present in every segment of the Polish housing market. Furthermore, this effect was stronger in secondary markets than in primary markets, as well as in the sales market, than in the rental market. However, the intensification of the endowment effect during the upward phase of the housing market cycle cannot be confirmed.

DOI: 10.1201/9781003512004-5

Future research directions and limitations

This book also provides a basis for future research on endowment effects in the housing market. First, in the empirical study in this book, as in other similar research, the explanatory power of the model for the WTA-WTP gap is not very high. Therefore, the factors shaping the WTA-WTP gap need to be explored further so that its identified size reflects the endowment effect as much as possible. Second, Chapter 2 provides additional theoretical predictions of the strength of the endowment effect for specific market situations: for the residential sublease market, during the buy-out of a dwelling by an existing tenant, when a party to a transaction changes the form of housing tenure, during the participation of real estate agents in the transaction, and when buyers/tenants are attached to the location of the dwellings being transacted. Further studies should attempt to verify the theoretical considerations presented in this regard. Moreover, because the endowment effect causes friction in the housing market and distorts the cleaning process, subsequent research should seek ways to minimise it or eliminate it altogether. Ultimately, future studies to fully understand the incidence of the endowment effect following loss aversion should try to empirically assess the importance of different reference points in the formation of WTA and WTP values.

The endowment effect study presented in Chapter 3 has several limitations. Similar to previous analyses in this area, it is based on stated preferences due to the unobservability of the WTA and especially WTP values. However, the intentions expressed by respondents do not necessarily translate into their actions. Further, to simplify the experiment, the inference on the strength of the endowment effect in secondary sales and rental housing markets was based only on transactions in which sellers/landlords treated housing as a consumption good. However, in these markets, sellers/landlords may also treat housing as an exchange good, as Chapter 2 points out. Depending on the number of transactions, the average strength of the endowment effect in the secondary sales and rental housing markets may be slightly lower than that reported in Chapter 3. However, one cannot claim a drastic change in view of the mean strength of the endowment effect estimated for primary housing markets. Some research limitations can also be noted in the context of the latter. This study assumes that the seller/landlord is a single human unit that determines WTA value. In the primary housing market, this situation may be true in many situations, but there are also cases where the WTA value is derived from the decisions of many individuals, especially in large housing developers.

Implications for policy

This study has several significant implications for policymakers. The government should aim to reduce the strength of the endowment effect to mitigate distortions in the housing market. Although the academic literature to date lacks positions strictly indicating how to do this, a starting point can be the considerations of Bao (2023), who proposed ways to support overcoming behavioural biases, leading to more rational decisions in the housing market. The first was education and awareness. With regard to the endowment effect, politicians using this tool should increase the availability of reliable information to the public on price development in the housing market. For example, Poland lacks an easy online platform that provides information on the transaction (not offer) prices of dwellings. Currently, this type of data is available at an aggregated level, that is, as average transaction prices in counties by quarters and made available by the Local Data Bank of the Central Statistical Office (https://bdl.stat.gov.pl/bdl/start). However, such a low level of detail for individual decision-makers in the housing market is insufficient to rationalise their actions. The second tool is visualisation, through which complex information can be processed more easily by people. In terms of the endowment effect, the visualisation tool can be combined with the previous one, that is, education and awareness, by adding to a potential house price online platform the possibility of visualising this data on a map. It should be noted that work on this started in Poland in 2023 under the name of the *Housing Price Portal,* and is currently being continued (Krześniak-Sajewicz, 2024).

The study in Chapter 3 indicated that the endowment effect is significantly smaller in the rental market than in the sales market. Therefore, from a macro perspective, policymakers' actions should aim to provide more support to this segment of the housing market. This is particularly the case in CEE countries, where there is a super-homeownership housing regime. The development of the rental market should result in an increase in housing affordability, as well as the stabilisation of the entire residential real estate sector, as also pointed out by other researchers (Rubaszek & Rubio, 2020).

The empirical findings of this monograph also indicate that during the up market, the WTA value is higher than the adopted benchmark, that is, the market price/rent of the property. This fact has highly significant implications for shaping legal legislation on residential property expropriation procedures. The latter usually assumes that compensation for the seized property is equal to its market value. However, when property owners' price expectations are higher than the market value, expropriation procedures can become inefficient and lead to conflicts between the government and the public. Therefore, the government should consider modifying expropriation procedures to consider the existence of the endowment effect so that the value of compensation is closer to the WTA value than the market value. In Poland, this type of solution is already in operation to some extent, for example, in the so-called *Special Road Legislation*, which aims at the efficient construction of public roads. Under this law, compensation for expropriated property is increased by 5% in relation to its market value when the real estate is released by the owner quickly, and by PLN 10,000 when it is a residential property. However, such regulations are overly general and should be specified across different segments of the housing market.

References

Bao, H. X. (2023). Between carrots and sticks, from intentions to actions: Behavioural interventions for housing decisions. *Housing, Theory and Society*. https://doi.org/10.1080/14036096.2023.2267060

Krześniak-Sajewicz, M. (2024). *Rząd PiS "nie dowiózł" ważnego projektu. Czy nowa władza pokaże, ile naprawdę kosztują mieszkania?* Interia. Retrieved February 29, 2024, from https://biznes.interia.pl/nieruchomosci/news-rzad-pis-nie-dowiozl-waznego-projektu-czy-nowa-wladza-pokaze,nId,7333749#google_vignette

Rubaszek, M., & Rubio, M. (2020). Does the rental housing market stabilize the economy? A micro and macro perspective. *Empirical Economics*, *59*(1), 233–257. https://doi.org/10.1007/s00181-019-01638-z

Index

Printed in the United States
by Baker & Taylor Publisher Services

Printed in the United States
by Baker & Taylor Publisher Services